FRANK O. GEHRY

FRANK O. GEHRY

INDIVIDUAL IMAGINATION AND CULTURAL CONSERVATISM

Edited by **CHARLES JENCKS** with a Critical Discourse by **ROBERT MAXWELL** and **JEFFREY KIPNIS**

A.D. ACADEMY EDITIONS

Acknowledgements

Unless otherwise stated, all photographic material is courtesy of either Frank O. Gehry and Associates or Charles Jencks; pp10, 11, 12 (above), 14 courtesy of Jo Reid and John Peck; p12 (below) courtesy of CZWG; p16 (above) courtesy of Jordi Sarra; p16 (below) courtesy of Tim Street-Porter; p18 (above) courtesy of Chris Gascoine; p18 (below) courtesy of José King; pp24-35 courtesy of Alsop and Störmer; pp48 (below) 50, 91 (above), 92 courtesy of Joshua M White; p49 courtesy of Architeckten Pfeifer and Associates; pp82, 84-85 courtesy of Thomas Dix.

Cover: The Guggenheim Museum, Bilbao, Spain, 1993-97
Page 2: Frank Gehry House, 1978

Edited by Charles Jencks

First published in Great Britain in 1995 by
ACADEMY EDITIONS

An imprint of
ACADEMY GROUP LTD
42 Leinster Gardens London W2 3AN
Member of the VCH Publishing Group

ISBN 1 85490 408 6

Distributed to the trade in the United States of America by
ST MARTIN'S PRESS
175 Fifth Avenue, New York, NY 10010

Printed and bound in Singapore

Contents

Frank O. Gehry

Creating Another Way

Charles Jencks

'I don't mind what you do, darling, so long as it's not on the street where it might frighten the horses.' This nineteenth-century Bostonian echoes Inigo Jones' pronouncements on building in the city: 'Ye exterior should be sober and rational, whereas ye interior can fly out licentiously'. The good Brit and Yankee are meant to be all pin-stripe sobriety on the outside while seething and outrageous on the inside, which brings me to Frank Gehry: he not only presents such contrasts in his architecture (on both sides of the facade) but he also makes a very convincing art from distorting familiar and sensible codes. With the recent completion of his American Center in Paris, and the Disney Hall under construction in Los Angeles, he is forcing the world to look again at the conflict between civic responsibility and individual creativity.

Gehry today is probably the number two architect in the world (first place being permanently unoccupied). His fame, influence and example extend from Patagonia to Vladivostok, his awkward collisions appear on most student draughting boards, and it is obviously only a matter of weeks before he appears on the cover of *Time*. We cannot avoid considering what he means for the customary opposition between conformity and individualism, ecological imperatives and personal expression, or – to give it the Eliotic formulation standard in literature – tradition and the individual talent. Are they opposed, synergetic, or mutually cancelling?

Gehry presents an unusual version of this conundrum. Born to Jewish parents in Toronto, Canada, in 1929, he has been influenced by this ethnic background. His architecture incorporates many recognisable and traditional elements, yet it always does so in a disguised or transformed way. The fish buildings and fish-scaled lamps, which started appearing in the 1980s were an intuitive response to the explicit quotes in Post-Modernism, that is they were recognisable

references to gefiltefishe and carp – the food of his Jewish upbringing – as well as being universal symbols and a reflection of architectural conventions. After migrating to LA where he studied art, then architecture, a very public persona was constructed of 'Gehry the architect'. Such reversals, such creative freedoms with traditions, *and* such doubts, are his hallmark. It has always been both bold and tentative.

It has also followed a clear development in spite of jumping from one idea and style to the next. His extraordinary accomplishment has been to be so creative and interesting for so long. Eero Saarinen, Paul Rudolph and Michael Graves – previous leaders of American architecture – remained creative for only a few years. Most architects repeat themselves out of necessity, as a conservative clientele typecasts their trademarks, demanding they repeat well-known formulae.

In this sense Gehry is rather the Picasso of architecture, picking up one new idea (and period) after another, grabbing anything and everything for his art, cannibalising high art and throw-away culture. In the early 1970s he gave architecture skewed perspectival space of a melancholic austerity, and elevated the wood stud skeleton, the staple of cheap building, into the 'cheap-skate aesthetic'. He also raised corrugated metal from the dead and by the late 70s, transformed chain-link fence into shimmering gauze. Countless other transformations were also lessons learned from the art world, so it *is* suitable that he should address artists and architects equally.

Like Picasso he is often best when slightly out of control, sketching freely again and again to uncover hidden meanings, or perhaps to transform failures to his purpose. His California Aerospace Museum visually annihilates the sub-classical building to which it is attached, but no one comments on this gruesome fact because his creation is such an intriguing explosion of abstract, awkward and representational shapes. Powerful sculptural creativity – which also works as cheap, functional architecture – disarms criticism.

Except perhaps, in Britain, where other more universal and conformist values often prevail. One finds the contemptuous attacks of Martin Pawley aimed at his reputation (the Vitra Centre is damned as a 'shoddy monster cottage' and 'mad munchkin' architecture) and the sceptical dismissals of Deyan Sudjic. These typify a certain spectrum of British opinion. The High-Tech and utilitarian approach has no use for the personal and expressive, any more than the classical and urban traditions of British architecture tolerate High-Tech. Indeed Gehry's individualism – like that of Will Alsop and Piers Gough whose work is also presented in this book – brings out the extent to which *any* tradition, whether civic, ecological, historical, economic or royal, is often pitted against personal creativity *per se*. Individualism is acceptable as long as no one can see it.

Despite occasional censure and loss of commissions, Gehry has continued to open new avenues of architecture, dragging reluctant critics along them. His village planning of the late 70s, like that of Leon Krier, established the small-block planning of the 80s. His *ad hoc* collisions of industrial building and Constructivist typology led, ten years later, to the Deconstructivist style. His 1988 vermiform museum for the Vitra furniture company in Germany, led to a resurgence of Baroque Expressionism – big fat curves immediately wriggled out through the student world, causing a plague of architectural worms. His fish and tree-like buildings have opened up the natural world as a source of the classical era. His heteromorphic compositions, which contrast one material and shape with another, have given birth to a whole school of LA urbanism.

In the long term, highly innovative architecture creates the very tradition by which it is judged. Such work underscores the paradox that it is only creative and disturbing architecture which has the power to engender tradition, keep it alive, and keep it from suffocating the parent that gave it birth. To a certain extent the more successful a creative architect, such as Antonio Gaudi, the more he will generate subsequent codes of perception and building codes which limit (as well as liberate) future generations. The individual imagination plays, in the long run, a culturally conservative role. Ponder the irony here: the innovative Inigo Jones and Robert Adam led to traditions of stasis and conservation.

The same is true of Mackintosh in Glasgow, Gaudi in Barcelona – and some day the very creative Gehry-*Schüle* in Los Angeles? Since any long-lasting city is a succession of such creative schools, frozen in stone by convention, we might approach the whole question of innovation with more tolerance and irony than we do.

But the architectural environment is perceived as a zero-sum game. If Prince Charles wins, High-Tech loses; if either of these two competing traditions dominate, then Post-Modernists are squeezed out; if they corner all the commercial jobs, then Modernists are unemployed; if the latter take control of the RIBA, then community architects are rendered obsolete. And so the power-go-round continues, with critics and architects shoring up their positions behind a fusillade of censure and ideology. Some of this may be necessary, some may be humorous, but the victim is usually the creative architect with an individual imagination. Very few people support the architectural imagination *per se*; so the architect is nudged towards one orthodoxy or another.

Gehry, and to a degree the other architects presented in this book and debate – Piers Gough and Will Alsop – have broken this perennial bind. They are mavericks, belonging to no obvious party (though they do have loyalties). Each is open-minded, each has cut out a space for individual creativity. In their own way, through example, each rebukes other architects for being too conformist. Collectively they – and the other architects I have discussed below under the rubric 'an architecture of pleasure' – are forging another way of creating. They, unlike other orthodox architects, are open about their artistic intentions, and the primary role speculation and modelling play. They make mistakes; they do not take themselves seriously all the time; they are humorous and they explore the unknown through painting, sculpture, graphics, pastiche, avant-gardism, commerce, and exploiting the vernacular. Their methods vary from the customary practice of architecture, and vary from each other. With Gehry's public success we have an architect, for the first time since Antonio Gaudi, who has re-set the balance between the individual and tradition clearly on the side of the individual. This shift, which is being followed by other designers such as Jean Nouvel, Nigel Coates, Phillipe Starck and Rem Koolhaas, may relocate international practice in the same directions. In any case, Frank Gehry's presence in Britain for the Fourth Annual Academy Architecture Lecture, June 11, 1994, became the challenge to ponder anew this fundamental balance.

Individual Imagination and Cultural Conservatism

An International Forum at the Royal Academy on the Occasion of Frank Gehry's delivery of the Fourth Academy Lecture, with Piers Gough and Will Alsop, June 11, 1994

This debate is often framed as a trade-off: more of one will mean less of the other. Especially after moments of economic and ecological crises, we face the politics of either/or. Today, because of economic and urban ills, because of pollution and mass extinctions, we again hear many calls to order, admonitions to build in regular ways, to return to conventions – the past – or perhaps to a future of mass-production. We hear valid claims for a green architecture, urban coherence and, in America, for 'an architecture of social responsibility'. In Germany, because of mass migration and ethnic tension, there is a call for uniform building and renovation rather than innovation.

These various programmes and calls to arms may be, at times, mutually exclusive, but invariably they run counter to the concept of pluralism and the imaginative creation of an expressive architecture. Here is also the negative-sum result that no individual or group really wants, the stalemate situation where all the valid public claims cancel out one another and a safe mediocre building – which no one likes – squeezes through as a political compromise.

The occasion of Frank Gehry's lecture – 'Since I'm So Democratic I Accept Conformists' – will set the framework for the debate. Gehry is probably the most successful imaginative architect practicing today with buildings rising throughout Europe and across America. Given the culturally conservative climate of Britain, it is hard to imagine him building here. British architects of his stature and inclination have had to work abroad, if they have wanted to build.

Yet the combination of imagination and cultural conservatism can be beneficial. After all, in the end everyone benefits from both an innovative architecture and a sustainable urban fabric. Indeed, in an important way these contrary institutions empower each other: as TS Eliot and the conservatives argue,

individual talent and freedom can only grow to any extent with, and through, a strong tradition.

There are entirely different justifications for supporting social welfare and those things we might share such as the city infrastructure. Under certain rare circumstances, such as those that prevailed in Florence during the Renaissance, or in Tokyo after the last war, we can find a positive-sum growth of individualism, and collective power can flower together and in part because of each other.

So the perennial debate continues – against the backdrop of whether we are in a positive-zero or negative-sum game, a synergetic or entropic situation – and it focuses on where and how we draw the lines and where we want the changing lines to point. There is no question, in an expanding pluralistic European culture, that these positions are always being renegotiated. So we have the limited choice of resetting the balance between individual imagination and cultural conservatism.

Charles Jencks

Paul Finch

In a nutshell, the subject for discussion this afternoon from a British perspective, is: 'how does Frank Gehry get away with it?' More formally, the session will concentrate upon how imaginative architects (particularly in Britain) find themselves operating in a situation of relative cultural conservatism. I suppose there may be a case for suggesting that the latter part of this statement is at least questionable, and we will no doubt move on to that.

It was recently remarked that since the patron lost his role as a stud, the architects now have to fertilise, and I suppose in Frank Gehry's case, 'fertilise in Vitra'. For those who have had the pleasure of seeing his work outside Basle will know that these are buildings of considerable power. Coming from Britain, I think we can ask why we do not build in such a way in this country.

I was struck by a remark of Pierre Chareau that in 1935 those who had money were not the kind of people the architects represented. This now has a sort of historical echo. So who does represent money in Britain and in other similar cultures today? It comes back to this question of individual aspects, the corporation, the public against the private, and the question of whether architecture is an useful icon for what is called 'the bespoke building' – which might be the future of offices in the City of London. Or whether it is a kind of function-sized economy, or just a question of doing the necessary with the minimum resources for those whose business it is to make investments which are incidental to architecture.

Another remark which struck me as relevant was Ettore Sottsass' statement that, 'if a society plans obsolescence, the only possible enduring design is one which comes to terms with that obsolescence'. That raises an interesting question. Although it is often said that we plan obsolescence, is it really true? The architects may acknowledge that critical essays which are written to describe their buildings will perhaps last longer than the buildings themselves – which is the critics' triumph, however nugatory, and the architects' tragedy – but I would suggest that there are very few architects who actually think about obsolescence in a serious way. On the other hand, there may be architects who stand precisely for obsolescence, but if they do, then what is society's attitude to such a proposition? Sottsass' question as to why it is thought that the pyramids are better than Burmese straw huts, seems to me to beg another question: 'who says they are better?' rather than simply saying: 'well, they are still around'.

Another question which is raised in Britain, as a result of the type of architecture Gehry designs, is why his 'equivalents' in this country seem to have to do so much of their work abroad or, if they attempt success in Britain, they seem to run into the inevitable problems encountered when entering competitions, which are failures for one reason or another – perhaps because they are too cynically organised or because financial backing does not really underlie the competition system.

We are going to begin this afternoon's event with a presentation by one of Britain's great imaginative architects. He may, however, disguise this when he is submitting the kind of drawings to a planning committee in order to cause the minimum fuss – I refer, of course, to Piers Gough. After tea we will have a presentation by

another architect who has produced a lot of work outside Britain in mainland Europe, Will Alsop.

Piers Gough

I am afraid I have not built anything much since the last time I spoke to you, because of the state of the world. But if somebody asks me to talk, I talk. Which in a funny way is similar to the question of individual imagination and cultural conservatism. Is architecture being asked to stand up and talk when it really has nothing to say?

The real dilemma is the subservience to the urban fabric, versus the desire to show the architect's individuality. We tend to work intuitively so I have never thought about it in that light, but what I realised was that my firm is the perfect definition of this dilemma because we try to do both at once, in every building.

China Wharf on one side tries very hard to be part of the street, although it is mannerist in its treatment of the vocabulary of the street. In other ways it is entirely un-mannered, in that it is built with the bricks used in the rest of the buildings in the vicinity; it has the same size windows, and so on. This is the desire to be polite, the desire to say: 'OK, we are part of a greater whole'. The other facade of the building kind of blows that idea because it wants to try and say something else, in this case, 'stop knocking down silos because they are beautiful' – although this does express a mannerist inversion.

The main area we have been concentrating on has been private housing. This is the most fraught area of architecture. It is one of those situations where you are building for somebody you have never met; you are building for a developer who wants to sell the property, and so that whole transaction is brought into architecture and your hope is that your client will think that your way of designing will attract people to buy. This is, of course, a very nebulous notion, and so you are designing buildings in a vacuum and trying to express both these ideas: the anonymity of living in the city versus the desire of everyone wanting to be an individual. The desire to be an individual is patently strong amongst the populace and the notion of living anonymously has weakened considerably. James Gowan said: 'The Prince wants to know how everyone in this country would like to live – and of course they would like to live in Kensington Palace'. If you were very rich you might build yourself a palace on the river, and so the notion is: why not live in a palace – an urban type of palace – on

Piers Gough – CZWG Architects, China Wharf, London

Piers Gough – CZWG, China Wharf, London

Piers Gough – CZWG Architects, Cascades, Docklands, London

the river? This was not previously available to anyone except the very wealthy. It seems to me an equally valid building type, so the point is that urbanity is consistent with anonymity, whilst also allowing certain people to demonstrate their importance – for example, the Church as it used to be. I suppose the big problem today is that nobody knows that urban place of private homes. Are they on the lowest rung? Are they on the bottom rung of architecture? Are they the most anonymous thing you can build, or are the big bureaucracies the most anonymous? What are we supposed to be celebrating now, since we do not go to church any more? We barely even go to the cinema.

As for buildings, how do we build them? Well, the horrible truth is we built them all in the Docklands, which is governed by a quango and does not have any voters to disagree with the planning committee's decisions. The truth is that we built what I think are probably stronger buildings, under a system which was not democratic. Docklands has a bad press. But it gave us a chance to build buildings which we considered worth building. In fact, I think Docklands is much maligned for its treatment of areas other than the central island on which Cascades stands. You can see we rather beat Canary Wharf to it, and the reason we had the opportunity to build this was the LDDC had a drawing with J Ware Travelsted saying he was going to build it. So we offered to build a footstool. The building is about anonymity: it is a repetitive building with each flat the same, one above the other. It is actually an extruded upright building, but on the other hand, because of its geometrical organisation of the big sloping south-facing side, we were able to make a lot of twists and incremental alterations to it, to give it a kind of inhabited quality; the quality of habitation beyond the obvious anonymity of exclusion. This building is all about that very balance between anonymity and individual expression within one structure, and perhaps we can therefore express this notion almost exquisitely in one building. The best article on this was: 'Castle Mythology in British Housing', in the RIBA Journal (Dec 1989). Obviously Cascades is not a palace, but it could be one.

The Circle in Bermondsey is another example of attempting to achieve both criteria at once. The individuality of the central urban space is counter-cultural – to date there are none of these tight circular spaces in the Docklands. I suppose it could be called an invention. It was designed as a piece of individual attention-grabbing space. We built an awful lot of London Stock bricks, built to continue the streets as they now find themselves, with a lot of windows more or less the same size (except they got bigger as they ascended the building). This graduation is ruthlessly rhythmical, as every window and every panel between each window are of identical widths all the way along the building – a very controlled exercise. Because we are who we are, we cannot resist moving balconies around to create a less calm facade. Behind this turmoil, however, is an anonymity, although the balconies are certainly expressions of habitation.

When the buildings at the Circle were sold, people bought the central blue ones first, although they turned out to be the most noisy. Due to the strong circular geometry, people are obviously going to drive in and go down to the car park at those points because that is where we chose to put the entrances. However, I was slightly shocked that rather than just live somewhere in the blue building, they actually wanted to live *behind* the blue bit. That says something about what people are looking for in housing beyond anonymity, they are looking for a certain feeling, a sense of being there and belonging to something that is noticeable, recognisable and identifiable. Of course, I like to think that we were also offering an urban space which was giving something back to the city. It was not just about building fancy facades for fancy people, there was a level of urban effort which was an extra space in the city – although of course, extremely compact in the way that area of Docklands is extremely compact.

When it comes to patrons and patronage, the great British architects are rarely employed because of the fear that as they are more famous than the person commissioning them, they will therefore run away with the budget. This would never change, as the press always supports the famous against the less famous poor-sucker client. One assumes that if one starts talking about patronage, one will frighten people: I think we *do* threaten. Architecture is already a threatening activity, and it is very dangerous to suggest that people have to rise higher in order to employ good architects.

Forms are sometimes laid over the anonymous to express individuality; but this often creates an architectural dilemma. This could be called the 'Janet factor', after an ordinary London house (for a woman called Janet) which has an overlaid form of what appears to be a fish (a homage to Frank Gehry). This is another example of individuality and the anonymous coming together in an attempt to express something acceptable, yet still a little different. Leading on from this overlaying of forms, there is the case of a private event taking place on a public facade – for example, Janet's little private breakfast balcony overhanging the street, where one can eat and observe the passers-by.

After twenty years of practice we were commissioned to design our first public building – a public lavatory. However, the commission was not from the local authority, but from the Pembridge Resident's Association, a pressure group for the re-Victorianising of the Pembridge area in Notting Hill Gate (as in putting back railings and balustrades and buying heritage lampposts). In commissioning us, on the advice of Terry Farrell, I think they surprised themselves. We rearranged the 'traffic island', which was not in fact a traffic island as we know it; there was no paving there at all, just a lot of parked cars and one portacabin lavatory. So we designed a building which stood on a very much larger piece of pavement, giving back to the community an area of greenery with benches and trees. The local residents thought it would be a good idea to have a florist's shop added into the brief *and* a clock *and* our fees, and still build it to the council's budget which would have been ideal, but in the end the residents had to pay for the clock and for the glass around the florist.

There is something raffish and bohemian about Westbourne Grove. If there is a dodgy hierarchy of building types now, then the building of public lavatories is certainly quite a new dilemma. Public lavatories tended to be anonymous and/or underground, but the notion of having extravagant public lavatories to celebrate some sort of civic pride has half the population saying to the Kensington and Chelsea council, 'why do you spend so much money?' while the other half says, 'why do you not do this every time'? I suppose they do not really know the answer to either question.

There were four attempts at getting the roof just right, and the end design is definitely the most picturesque, as it has a curved, rather than square-ended roof. (Incidentally, for a building like this, you first receive planning permission; and only then do you send in the colour of brick you are thinking of using – you have to take one step at a time, in the hope that the authorities have devolved the power of choosing the brick to the planning officer.) Thank you.

Piers Gough – CZWG Architects, The Circle, Bermondsey, London

Robert Maxwell

I am very glad that Piers' work is on show today because I have a feeling that on seeing it Frank will suddenly decide that after all there is some hope for this country, as it certainly stands out! You know it is true that people do not like you here if you stand out too much – even more if you are like Frank, getting all the commissions. Everyone I spoke to on a recent American trip said 'Frank's at it again, he is terrible', and this is obviously a mark of the competitive spirit they have there. In this country we know who gets virtually every commission going – I have not heard anybody say 'Norman [Foster] again?'

Frank Gehry

I was jealous that he got Janet's house because she is my friend!

Robert Maxwell

That again says there is hope that you are in some kind of free-moving continuum. Over here it is all too close to what Charles Jencks describes as a game, which is to say that you have to choose: either you are High-Tech or you are a Classical Revivalist. In either case you are going to have backing, and hope that your side will win, but you do not want to be in the middle where you get squeezed. That is the reaction I get and I hope that I am not being too Presbyterian in suggesting that there is a terrible conformity in England today. We really need to address this issue in order to find out if 'we have space for an individual'. Is it right that everything should be the same, or is it right that most places should be the same but a few places should be different – which would not be too bad a compromise. In that sense I really have to say that I enjoy Piers' immodesty. On the English scene, it is refreshing. Why is Colin Rowe going back to America? The public meaning is that he cannot bear to live under a monarchy. Of course we know there are private reasons as well, but the very fact that he can give that reason tells us something. I know that this is the Royal Academy of Art, I know that we have royalty and I know that not everybody shares my sentiments – I am not really talking about politics, I am talking about climate, the climate of conformity, the unwillingness to accept something weird. I hope a degree of toleration will gradually come to be extended outside the walls of 34 Bedford Square.

Paul Finch

Well I know that there is someone who thinks that Sir Norman Foster gets too much work. This someone is OM Ungers, whom I met recently, and who told me that *Der Spiegel* had just carried out an interview with Foster in which the latter was very complimentary about how generous the Germans were to let a British architect design their central government building. Ungers' point was that yes, it was generous, but why are the Germans being so generous when no one has asked *him* to do anything in London – or, in fact, anything in Germany?

Perhaps Alan Balfour would like to comment on how he sees this rise of High-Tech or Classical Revival from his perspective, both at the AA and after his long experience in America? I was wondering if his view of what was going on here has been tempered or modified over the last three or four years.

Alan Balfour

Well, I am struck by Bob's comment about the reason for deference. When I arrived at the opening of Prince Charles' new school, all fifty of us were kept by the garden fence, and I had a distinct sense of suddenly shifting from being a citizen to being a subject. Indeed, the notion of being a subject is certainly present in the British imagination. The extraordinary freedom in Frank's work seems to me to oppose and distance itself from our context. We appear to find it very difficult to do the kind of thing he does, it seems to be an immensely difficult task for our imagination. How does one escape from it? We are increasingly driven to capitalise on history to somehow see it enforce a piece of the cultural imagination which lies in romantic objects. It continues to re-invent the notions of Regency life – notions of medieval mysteries are of much more power here than notions of the future. The burden of cultural constraint is imposed upon us. There is a potential breakthrough to our increasingly international situation but it also fails to touch the ground, by increasingly pushing the imagination and divorcing it from context. In all this I sense there is a cultural burden on our imagination, from which we almost have to wilfully distance ourselves.

Robert Maxwell

What Alan has just said very interesting, because it brings up a certain question of framing. When Piers described his building, he mentioned that parts of the building face the street and that these are the

Piers Gough – CZWG Architects, FROM ABOVE: The Circle, Bermondsey, London; Janet Street-Porter's House, Barbican, London

conventional parts, whilst the other parts are more impolite, individualistic and excessive. One might say the same about the American Center in Paris, where some parts are polite and others are less polite. In his case, Piers has taken within himself the whole business of mediating the burden of history and tradition and is now offering a new amalgam, where somehow or other we are encouraged to accept something new when it is put into a familiar situation. I do not know whether Piers would like to comment on that, whereas I suspect that Will will give us more about total offering, which is a hard sell offered up against the status quo. There are two different ways of balancing it here: whether the architect takes on the burden of mediation or whether he plays it very hard in the hope that he will puncture the pomposity just by driving a hard arrow through the edges. I realise why the High-Tech approach is so much preferred in this country – there is a lot of self expression in it, but you offer it entirely as a service, and that sort of alibi makes us comfortable. I am offering this line of thought, but I would like to know what Piers thinks.

Piers Gough

I feel it is a weakness, because I feel this overreaction action between context and knowing the city is superficial for a start, as I do not do the kind of in-depth studies of what the real underlying city is. I tend to be someone who just knows what Notting Hill Gate is like because I have lived there, it is too predictable. In a way I do not like it, it is like being too sensitive, too complex, too understanding of what is going on, and really not being bloody-minded enough. However, we do get these buildings up, so there is a ghastly equation of successfully building rather than not building. We recently won five out of six limited competitions. I look back now and think: 'how could we?' It is almost disgusting, because it just shows we have bought ourselves off; we have made ourselves able to just get the timing right so that we are neither too dangerous nor too safe, we are just exactly what people want in architecture, which is just enough new that is going to be comfortable, and that they can cope with. I feel that is not pushing the culture hard enough our way. When I was younger I used to think that I wanted to be a baroque or mannerist architect. I wanted to take things and alter them, using all the appropriate vocabularies and parts, but now I feel there is something more, and that possibly the lack of freedom of our buildings – the sort of uptight quality of the symmetries – demonstrates slightly too clearly that sculpturability is not there. That is why, I suppose, Frank is a long way ahead in my mind because he not only does things we do, but he does them as a sort of by-product of a freer spirited, more determined desire to build certain kinds of buildings which nobody is asking Frank to have invented anyway.

Frank Gehry

The context in which I grew up in California is not the historic context, so when my work is photographed it is usually done without the context. Europeans who have seen pictures of the buildings do not see what is around them, and do not see that it is a very contextual building in a very traditional sense. I bought in the same things you did, except mine are weird, because it is a chaotic environment made from some kind of new government called democracy. I think the reason some of the French journalists have been knocking my building in Paris as not being 'real Frank Gehry' is because this building is purposefully concerned with a lot of my feelings about Paris. I play Paris, I love Paris, I make love to Paris with the American Center, and they do not like it. I do not think the context is a bad thing to deal with, in fact it is almost a deal with the social structure, with what has gone on before.

Piers Gough

I think the problem is that the context is not intellectual. It does not move the culture in the same way.

Frank Gehry

It is in a sense if you look at it as sculpture: it forms in space, trading spaces. Look at it this way: it is like a chess game with you making the next move on the table, and by making this next move you make the whole better. It is my fancy you are making the whole better than it was, and if it is appropriate, you steal centre stage. If it is in the case of something like a concert hall, I feel that is appropriate. I do not remember where I did *not* feel it was appropriate.

Robert Maxwell

So if it is appropriate, that means you have a sense of limits, such as whether you tell a certain story at a certain dinner party, but not at another dinner party. Tact is not appropriate for a member of the avante-garde. I would like to ask Will if he would like to come into this particular exchange – do you think that in your buildings there is a certain compromise with some tradition, maybe the tradition of modernity? Or is it nothing but out and out steel arrows thrust at humanity?

Will Alsop

Looking at Piers' work, it struck me that there was an essential difference. I admire his work tremendously and I think clients commission Piers because they like him; actually love Piers to a certain extent. It might not be true, but that is the way I perceive it, and there is a certain connection between Piers and London which I think is very touching and very important to the whole of Europe. Clients come to us, not because they love us, but because they do not intend to come to us – a lot of our work used to come through competitions, but that is beginning to change now because they can see there is evidence of this stuff. I do not feel constrained by any notion of context; of what architecture *should* be or by any notion of good manners. Indeed, I rather enjoy bad manners, which sometimes gets me into trouble – I lost a client on Thursday in Edinburgh through opening my mouth! On the other hand, you watch TV and that extraordinary interview with Melvyn Bragg and Dennis Potter, who knew he was going to die. He was saying everything he wanted to say with touching honesty. In a way it is that honesty that could save the world.

Paul Finch

Thus, most clients or client bodies seem to want something which is safe – they might like some *frisson*, but not too much. But why is it that only architecture is affected by this? In a variety of other areas, for example music, theatre and the fine arts, there does not seem to be this problem about cultural conservatism.

Max Hutchinson

I particularly like Will's point about the fact that with people like Piers (and if Piers picks up the phone and says that CZWG wants to obtain a planning application in a certain borough, it is certain that something big is going to happen) it is going to be different, and they can take it or leave it. As Piers knows, I do not like his buildings, or actually, to use the past tense, did not like his buildings. About three weeks ago the BBC rang at about 11.50am and said that as Piers had not turned up, they were wondering if I could talk for half-an-hour about a public toilet that had just won an award. I

Piers Gough – CZWG Architects, Westbourne Grove Public Lavatories, London

jumped in a cab and went off to the BBC and thought on the way, read the press cuttings, looked at the picture and said, 'that is fantastic, I am so glad this toilet has happened'. I suddenly understood why I was glad it had happened and what I would have done, had I done it. It would have been white and would have had white louvres. It was not white and did not have louvres; and it had got planning consent. It also had flowers about it, so I thought, 'I pass the Janet Street Porter house almost every day because I live in the Barbican, and I'm a "street vegetarian". I wear black and white, so to walk past Janet Street Porter's house is actually quite a style statement for me. I don't go and snog in the park'. I suddenly realised that what I liked about the toilet was the Ealing comedy aspect of Piers' architecture, the sort of Norman Wisdom of it all, and when Piers describes it, I wish he would smile a bit more because now when I see it like that, I see a humorous gesture. It is a sort of *Four Weddings and a Funeral* architecture – we can see layers of irony, teasing and English meaning. I cannot dismiss it from its context, nor its Englishness which lurks behind the facade of the Georgian house or the Banqueting House of Inigo Jones. It relates to what Pevsner described as the 'Englishness of English art', which is so complex and ironic. Maybe Piers would be a little bit pleased that now I can laugh and enjoy.

I do remember one agonising moment when some TV interviewer, who was far too intellectual for his own good, as well as very good looking, asked me to justify Cascades. One of the ironies about Cascades is that the patron (the owner of Kentish homes) went bust after having poured a lot of money into it. I think the interviewer asked what this building was about and I coined some odious phrase to justify its context in the moving continuum of the Docklands. Now I find myself smiling about it and saying, 'well there is only one Piers Gough, there is only one blue-clad circle in Docklands and there is only one Janet Street Porter's house. I can have as much as Piers can do for as long as he is here'.

Paul Finch

But what about this other question, about conservatism in respect to other art forms? You are very heavily involved in music; what is the problem here?

Roger Zogolovitch

I think that to answer your question specifically you have got to look at the length of the audience. The difference between architecture and the performance of architecture, and musical architecture and filming, is that film-making borders those other mediums on a direct link with the audience. You know whether a film is successful or unsuccessful because ten billion butts go and sit on seats throughout the world. The money lender may have difficulty in translating that into a return, which is entirely to do with the creativity of the art which has just been seen. We have an element of populism in some aspects: for example, in museums or public buildings where the architecture actually and suddenly speaks to you. I was recently asked about the Pompidou Centre, and I asked the guy from Paris if he could tell me whether anybody has ever examined the numbers beneath the economic benefit or the economic depreciation that has taken place. The numbers have suddenly changed as a consequence of that building.

I think that half our problem here is that the mechanism of judging our medium in financial terms is limited, since you are confined to the issue of ownership when you are trying to reflect something which Piers discussed regarding the palazzo. There is no longer a notion of a palazzo; what we have in our society is a notion which millions pay a dollar to go through.

Jeff Kipnis

I was watching the Trooping of the Colour this morning and comparing it to the New York Macy's Thanksgiving Day parade. I think the differences between these two parades bear on the issues we are exploring this afternoon. The Trooping of the Colour has a high level of regimental order and a familiar historical typology. Idiosyncracies are allowed, such as the Duke of Kent riding a grey horse against a brace of black horses, to express a simple, even dialectical difference. This is precisely what appears to be happening in Piers' work. Piers accepts a limited set of typologies of acceptable urban form. Within this given set, he expresses a small attitude of idiosyncrasy but basically works within very familiar typologies of urban space, architectural space and architectural form.

On the other hand, in the Macy's parade, an entirely different and infinitely more complex order is in evidence. Every element is different, incongruently related to one another in form, scale, location in space, organisation geometry and so on. These incongruencies do not lapse into mere incoherence. Rather, they indicate a new spatial order, the predecessor to a new

type of space – social, organisational and urban. The difference between Piers' work and Frank's work is parallel to the difference between the Duke of Kent in the Trooping of the Colour and the ordered incongruity of Macy's parade. Piers is interested in an idiosyncracy that singles out individuality but confirms familiar typology of community order, while Frank seems more interested in pursuing a fundamental, new approach to community order.

I think such an approach misses a fundamental point in the transformative capability of architecture that can be learnt, for example, from Frank's work. His work is not about idiosyncratic individuality against the anonymous background of standard types of community, it is about a new community constructed out of idiosyncracies. Perhaps LA is the most extreme case, but it is characteristic of American cities, in that the community is constructed out of a fabric of idiosyncrasy rather than individualist idiosyncrasy against community.

Secondly, it is hard to find simple ornamentation in Frank's work; in fact, unlike Piers' work, I think one would be hard pressed to locate in the former's work what is ornament and what is not. The idiosyncrasy is facial, formal, and material. Hence, I do not think it is appropriate to state that Frank's work, like Piers' is simply a discussion about expression and freedom versus the boredom of the norm, nor is it just about re-stating familiar types and then making them more interesting. Frank's work possesses a transformative vocation. So when I hear Piers' comment about a desire to transform public space and then I see him apply familiar typology about what constitutes public space, I am disturbed. Compare his treatment of the housing on the roundabout with Frank's work at Vitra. Grimshaw had set up a very interesting regimentation; then Frank designed a museum which could have stood out in sculptural difference. Instead he used the staircases to completely transform the organisational character of the site by intergrating his sculptural museum to Grimshaw's regimentation.

Our discussion can become more interesting if we do not simply fall into these dialectic terms of same and difference, or familiar patterns of order and ornamental expressions of difference, but look at the architectural capacity to transform typology, with an understanding that you do not simply abandon the history of order and of typology.

Robert Maxwell

It seems that the way things get transformed within history is by a process of assimilation.

Piers Gough

One forgets about working in London, even for the smart guys who built the *Channel 4* building, but in actual fact they merely furnished the Victoriancy, and that is what you are doing. London is here, it has streets and we are not about to move them – in fact the only time we tried to change the South Bank we put some streets in the air, and suddenly a decision was taken to pull down the complex. There is no willingness for transformation, and *that* is the essence of it. I am part of it, I agree, I am not pushing at the door and saying it is time we transformed a city. We have not done anything to transform it in your terms, there is just nobody here who has managed to transform the city. We rediscovered the Victorian city, decided not to knock it down, and have decided to go along with it because it is here, and because it has got the sewers.

Jeff Kipnis

Let me suggest that you are not transforming it but are actually affirming it. I am simply subscribing to your own self-criticism and perhaps trying to make it a little more naked. You concretise the existing order by essentially participating in its larger ordering principles and then using small scale material and ornamental gestures to make that participation slightly more interesting. I would also like to underscore Frank's own criticism of his work in Paris. I believe that work is disappointing compared to his other work, precisely because he assumes there was such as thing as Paris, and then simply tweaked that existing situation. Hence, I think the fundamental responsibility of architecture both at the building level and at the urban level is to assess what the state of community is, the individual in relationship to community, and then find a way to operate upon it at the spatial level and not merely at the expressive level.

Charles Jencks

How does the new, shocking part of a city relate to the old part, culturally? I was being driven around La Défense by Rem Koolhaas, and I said, 'you cannot really defend this giant modern development?' He replied: 'it kept the rest of Paris from being destroyed'. That is what Leon Krier proposed when he said 'true plurality (as opposed to false pluralism) consists in connecting the old city with the new by a bridge to give a real choice'.

La Défense is a free-fire zone of new building which keeps old Paris intact. True pluralism is about choice. Secondly, the European community has brought up the importance of the culture of the *nouveaux-riches* as patrons, and the dominance of the market place. In America, there is a very strong market-oriented culture; in fourteenth-century Venice the *nouveaux-riches* were building palaces – fifteen miles of them – which we now call the Grand Canal, and consider to be the greatest sequence of architecture ever created.

It is unthinkable that architecture on this scale happens outside the *nouveau-riche* culture, because they are the ones who want to establish their identity. The Venetians, according to the historian John Onians, as good Christians read the Biblical injunctions to avoid architects. Christians had to be against personal expression in architecture, so the Venetians salved their guilt by writing on their buildings in Latin – 'For the Glory of God'.

Robert Maxwell

Well Jeff, where is transformative architecture that shows what it can do?

Jeff Kipnis

I think in Frank's best work we can look at an architecture which moves from the idiosyncratic to the transformative. One example is a close analysis of the Disney project, which will prove to show that it virtually has nothing to do with mere sculpture against the background setting, but is a real urban project which shows something well beyond its symbolic and aesthetic character when establishing the character of the urban space and also the urban community.

Robert Maxwell

So Disney will be an example of transformative architecture?

Jeff Kipnis

If you look at the space of the Macy's Parade, you see highly incongruent objects, multiple materials and sculptural disorder. However, you have to be able to recognise that the Macy's Parade is not just disorder, but latent order that can be physicalised, and I think that is what Frank is doing at Disney.

Robert Maxwell

So Frank's architecture is an example of transformative architecture?

Jeff Kipnis

In some projects, yes.

Kevin Rhowbotham

This personality issue is also cultural conservatism of the most profound kind. Architecture closes out the operation of individuals by electing its own representatives who confine themselves to certain kinds of legitimation. Regarding the rather interesting point about this transformation spatiality, I would like to know how it might constitute anything other than the kind of Victorian functionalist spatiality. What I do not see is any mechanism for representing an alternative spatiality within the confines of architecture at the moment. There is none – if we ask for a critical, political, or psychological spatiality, I cannot accept that there is any architect anywhere, apart from myself, who has even attempted to construct a representational approach to an alternative spatiality.

Kevin Rhowbotham

But these are special arcane arguments which seem to me to have no purchase on general political interests in the nature of spatiality and freedom.

Roger Zogolovitch

What we have not mentioned here is the issue of the British class system. The architect has to attain a notion of popular appeal. If you ask the public to state their favourite street in the world, they may well say, for example, 'Marlborough High Street', but then if you ask the same people whether there is a McDonald's in Marlborough High Street, they ask you what you mean, because in that knowledge of the picturesque they immediately edit out McDonald's from the context in which it really exists. In America they do not have that. They will tell you whether there is a McDonald's or a Burger King or anything else. I think the strange thing is that we are doing the same editing in terms of the City of London, as we do not look at the edges of it: such as the Westway which plunges out from Marylebone Road and creates extraordinary urban spaces which have no language to them, and which are waiting for the transformation that Jeff has been speaking of. We do not

actually use the territory of our cities to make it a part of a language that could introduce a new form of architecture

Robert Maxwell

You have actually given the reason why so many student projects over the last fifty years have been situated in and around motorways, because that is the leftover space that does not fit into the accepted structure of the city. But one could also say that it is leftover space created after an act of engineering which was not intended ever to be social.

Roger Zogolovitch

It is not just the leftover space, it is actually part of the city. It is very different from the elements that Piers was picking up of the Victorian city that the rest of us are trying to hatch in. Hence, if you are presenting in political terms what you are discussing, and are standing in front of a Planning Committee or the Royal Fine Arts Commission or whoever, and they are asking you why you should build a three-storey Victorian red brick building when you are actually trying to face up to an engineering structure opposite, which is only four stories in the air – what is the context? It may be something which can only be resolved by invention and imagination.

Jeff Walker

I think editing is a key to a lot of this. I have been re-reading texts by men such as Gropius and Pevsner, who told us that for architecture to be socially responsible it has to be rectangular, flat and dull grey, and that anything else is socially irresponsible. In 1936, Pevsner for instance, claimed that Gropius' Fagus Factory was the model of twentieth-century architecture, and anything that departs from that is wrong. In 1960 he initially said that things were going badly wrong again because of Le Corbusier's Ronchamp, and the Brazilians who were building all their sculptural stuff. Pevsner believed that architecture was taking a wrong turning and ever since then there have been people calling for a return to order. I think the Neo-Rationalists did that a little in the 70s and it happened when Ken Frampton wrote about critical regionalism with three preferred examples: Siza, Botta and Alagan. The trouble is with the people who read the magazines and who judge a competition. They have their agenda for what architecture should be, and reject the ideas they do not like. The intriguing thing about Piers Gough's loo is that the Continental magazines showed the geometric element because that is what they are looking for, whilst the English magazines showed the High-Tech element, a product of the editors at work.

Tony Fretton

In some places there is a tendency to find a collective realisation of the city; a consequence of cultural attitudes and activity. In Amsterdam, for example, the centre of the city has been meticulously preserved physically, but you only have to look through windows to see that the interior has been utterly transformed. It is full of the original activities that made it what it is, and even if its preservation passed the time of its original authenticity, it is a change which in a sense is outside architecture. It is to do with cultural attitudes. Picking up Jeff's point that cities are a much broader collectively realised activity (which I think is evident in every park) and that is why it has happened in artists such as Frank - I have seen his work touching on areas of what architecture should look like. It seems Frank's work has reference to objects of production as much as architecture. This is very exciting as it relocates architecture back in industrial society in a way that architects will choose to avoid seeing.

Robert Maxwell

I think that Tony has put his finger on something here because when we talk about the city we are not just talking about physical space, we are talking about the use of that space, about a very varied clientel. I am thinking about the time when we had a housing scheme; it was selected to be decorated with a piece of sculpture, and to ensure that it was not too pompous we collaborated with an artist to have it as play sculpture. It turned out to be a little daisy wheel in welded steel on two or three levels, which kids could fall off and not hurt themselves. It also looked nice from above. What we did not realise was that it was situated on green space which we had carefully won by tucking the garage underneath, and when the kids from the next estate came over and played steel band on it, it reverberated! They came over every night, playing to a point where the sculpture had to be demolished and taken away. We certainly did not anticipate that – we anticipated where the kids would drop off onto the ground and we put astro turf there instead of natural grass, but we did not think the kids in

the next estate would play their steel band on it and create a nuisance. The point is that a city is made up of people who are not equal in their appreciation of art. An example of this is Serra's 'Tilted Arc' in Manhattan, which was a very sensitive piece of wall sculpture.

Rosalind Krauss wrote that it actually created a new sense of spatiality, but it had to be taken away because the local residents objected to it as it stopped them walking directly across the square. That does not mean that it was not a great piece of art; it just means that if you put a piece of art across a certain position in public it will be seen as a barrier. So we have these multiple references.

Another point I want to make is on a book by Paul Hersh, in which he points out that there are two kinds of property – non-positional and positional: if you have a TV it does not inhibit your neighbour from having one; if you watch a certain television programme, it does not inhibit your neighbour from watching other programmes; but if you own a villa on a lakeside you stop everybody else from having a villa on that particular site. So architecture is positional, and by taking possession of the ground you are unavoidably creating a political situation – and that is where the whole public row comes out. Charles was citing the success of the Burgher Houses in Amsterdam, all different and individual yet almost the same, because they are conforming to a taste ethos. The same can be said about the Bedford Street estate in London, where the appearance of each building is identical to the next because it was servicing a class, all of whom wanted to be identified as gentlemen. However, you do get moments in history when you get that kind of collusion between an upcoming player – the *nouveaux-riche* – and the settled convention. The convention is adopted as the key to their acceptance in society. That illustrates that society is very much made up of social classes and emphasises the steps by which conventions stabilise the system for a time. Transformational architecture appears to refuse any rigorous logical or historic argument, on the hope that whatever transformation is offered, it will in due time become the status quo.

Jeff Kipnis

Of course the element of transformation is precisely that. Is not the point of architecture always to imagine a new order, new social arrangements, new institutional forms, and not merely to criticise the existing?

Piers Gough

In truth I see that London is not just going to be transformed – that may be a pathetic view but then I look at Berlin which refuses to transform itself, determined to continue as a Victorian city. Berlin has the opportunity to rebuild itself and if I have personally done anything to prompt Berliners to feel they do not have to consider transformation – which I feel perhaps I have – I regret it. But I maintain they are letting a tremendous opportunity slip through their fingers.

Paul Finch

A lot of people have been saying that Norman gets too much work, so there is no better person to kick off with than Will Alsop, who, as I am sure you are aware, was the last person to beat Norman, in the competition for the hotel in Marseilles, which is nearly completed.

Will Alsop

I felt that earlier we were sort of consumed by eloquence. Sometimes eloquence does consume a certain sensibility, and there is a very obvious rift between those like me who actually make the stuff together with the frame, and Piers and his type, who actually write about it and think about it. It struck me that perhaps the obstruction could well be the media, for some types of architecture and planning are opposed to the local authority. It could be that I am just getting older! I remember Robert Maxwell chairing a conceptual architecture conference in 1974, and I thought he spoke extremely well; it was interesting to hear him say that as he has got older he has become more conservative. I suppose the answer is, 'so have I', but nevertheless the gap remains the same. There was a time in this country – perhaps fifteen years ago – when if you had gone to see a planner with a scheme in mind, and they had said, 'yes, that's marvellous', you would have been embarrassed as you obviously had failed to do the job properly. To put it very simply, I think it can be put down to the fact that people who are getting into power in the planning department are the ones who took drugs – and there is a big difference between the pre- and post-drug people. I have noticed it, I no longer have the same problems, and life is much easier. Berlin is difficult – my theory is that they have *all* been taking drugs.

Charles Jencks

Koolhaas made much the same point.

Will Alsop

Yes, I am frightened that when I am in late life (assuming that I make it to a great age), my children will be in power, and they are terrible.

However I am now going to return to the subject of Berlin. It is very difficult to know quite where to start on this occasion – as it always is – but particularly with the people who are gathered together in this room. In Berlin we are constructing a building which for me is quite difficult because I cannot actually show you what it looks like. The architecture is evolving in such a way that I cannot draw it. I think that is quite interesting, it is one of those passions that I have and I attempt to ensure that it is interesting to anyone else. However, I appreciate it is particularly hard for the client when he asks what it looks like, and I cannot give him a straight answer. It is also hard for the planners who state that planning permission is going to take eighteen months – a long time, even by London standards – for a building of some fifteen or sixteen thousand square metres. This continues until the planner (you know that she is a member of the green party because she has a green band in her hair) suddenly says, 'well 400,000 DMs for a bit of sculpture in front of Martin Gropius wouldn't go amiss really'. So we all really lie in a way. It does not matter who you are, there is always a certain element of lying in order to get what you want, and I think it would be foolish to pretend otherwise. We invent ways of dealing with the bureaucracy because as architects, and being members of a race which are hated very often (but loved in Piers' case) you have to find ways to make people love you, or at least get worried about something else other than you.

I think it is important to make one's position as an architect fairly clear. I know I have used this before (and I make no apology for using it again), but it was William Butler Yeats who said 'in dreams begin responsibilities'; I believe it is our responsibility to have those dreams. I would like to make it absolutely clear that I *do* regard myself as an individual, and that individuality is something that differentiates me from the rest of the world. Thank God not everybody is like me, and I am not like the rest of the world. Although that might sound a little bit arrogant, it does mean that I feel a duty, duty being an important word to explore that individuality; to realise that there are perhaps ways which I can not always evaluate or indeed always articulate. For me everything that we do is part of one work, and that one

Will Alsop – Alsop and Störmer Architects, FROM ABOVE: Sylt-Quelle, Germany; Kunstverein, Hamburg; Visitor's Centre, Cardiff

work is made up of a number of different aspirations, and to a certain extent it does not matter if they are built works or un-built works. One uses each project to rediscover another aspect of what one is doing in oneself. I make no apology for that. Architects change throughout their working life, and I think it is important to remember that they do not confirm things – they confuse things in the most useful sense; this is our job.

With regard to the building in Marseilles which Paul referred to, it is noticeable that it is the only blue building in Marseilles. It deliberately does not fit into any context. The person who is responsible for changing the way we think about our cities is the traffic planner. He has immense power in comparison to even the civil engineers and architects, as he is *listened* to.

The other important element which this project displays is our approach to work. On one level it can be said that we work in a very similar way to a painter or sculptor – we inform. What I am primarily interested in is the idea of compromise and how, by making a proposition, you can actually begin to use the comments of other people – the team that one is working with, whether it is the engineers or the client themselves – to draw them into the conversation about what it is you are attempting to achieve. This is one of the great disadvantages of competitions, they do not allow client body involvement in conversation. Catalysing the people who are responsible in one form or another for the creation of a building is extremely hard, and because of this I have become far more open minded towards the work of other architects – provided they go through the process with commitment. I can hate the work, love what they do and love them, and I think that is a critical point for me, as a critical shift from 1974 to now, because I demand freedom to make what I want in the method that I choose, and the method that I choose is one of compromise.

We have lost some battles and won others, but that is the way it is and that is what I enjoy, since that way one can actually achieve. You start out by saying, 'I don't know what we are going to do'. You are therefore giving your client – or the planner or politicians – the same problems that you have, and in this way they share the experience of why and what you could do.

The product of an idea can sometimes be a problem. One particular architect had an idea that a rock concert hall would be interesting if it looked like the top of a skull – preferably bald – with headphones. The bands that play there have nothing to do with the structure at all, it is there because the architect was required to literally build his vision.

One of the features about working in France is that the French see architecture as part of culture and, to them, culture is very important. Hence, they are very curious about what the architect's concept is, and the Marseilles project was an example where lying was required, because there was no concept *per se*; there was the concept about the process and evolution of the project, but there was no sort of grand notion behind what this building should *be*. Hence I had to lie, and talk about the relationship between the blue and democracy of the building all of which are there, but they are not the motivating force behind making the project work.

We were asked to design and build a water-bottling plant in Sylt in northern Germany. There was a requirement that it should look like a lighthouse – that is what the local burgomaster stated – so to save disappointing him we designed a lighthouse. Another requirement was to use a certain quantity of bricks, so we fulfilled this wish as well.

It is also very nice to work on existing buildings, such as the Institute of Contemporary Arts in Hamburg, which was converted from a fruit market gallery and has worked out quite well. It is good to discover new use, as it brings new behaviour into this particular part of the city. Of course you could look at that the other way round; the context of the city is perhaps not the context that we should be looking at. On one level you have Patrice Goule saying that one of the most fantastic things about Marseilles is the elevated highway that swings around over the harbour and brings you down into the old port – it is one of the best ways to arrive in any city in the world, and in this case the intervention has been carried out very bravely, with some of the supports actually running through the middle of the existing buildings. This is quite an extraordinary achievement, as layer after layer rests one on another. On the other hand, it has destroyed vast parts of the city, which have consequently been shifted out beyond the city boundaries and have therefore colonised what were formally more rural areas. Thus, people leap-frog out beyond that and then, before you know it Marseilles is the same as Aix-en-Provence. Hence we get very large, not exactly urban, not exactly sub-urban, and not exactly rural areas. I personally rather like this undefined city.

Someone was talking about planned obsolescence

earlier on. It is rather interesting that I, too, was rung by the BBC – not to talk about the lavatory, but to be on one of these *Building Sights* programmes. They asked me what ideally I would like to do: it had to be in the UK and it had to be twentieth century, and I said I would rather like to do Cedric's interaction building in Kentish Town. This displayed a particular way of thinking which obviously disappointed them profoundly – I asked what the matter was, and they explained that it is a bit ugly. That is very interesting – you can use the word 'ugly' in this context, but it is difficult to use the word 'beauty' or 'beautiful'. The irony of the building in Cardiff was that I had to get planning permission, even though it was temporary and this created difficulties. People say, 'well it looks a bit funny, it looks a bit weird', but now that it has been there for three or four years and the plan is to build a more permanent structure on this site (not by us), the people of Cardiff consider it a landmark and want to keep it. To move it 400 metres around the bay and then to upgrade it to give it a longer life will cost more than the original cost of building. This is where the difficulties take place regarding planning conditions, with obstructions cropping up continuously. In spite of what I said about planning officers, not all of them have taken drugs yet. What you find, I think, is that there has been a general shift since 1968, with the whole process of planning becoming increasingly political. This has been an obstruction to many of what I consider an extraordinary collection of talented architects in this country (and particularly in London). The politicians no longer trust their planners, so they make the decisions themselves; the planners consequently feel that they cannot make strong recommendations to their members. It would be good to do something about that.

Piers Gough

My view is that that is Prince Charles' main legacy.

Will Alsop

I agree with you.

Piers Gough

Do not trust professionals, follow your own direction.

Will Alsop

The whole issue of Prince Charles' beliefs has its advantages and disadvantages, but more of that later.

You find that you build places in funny places. We

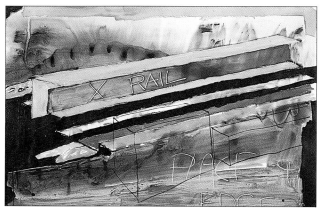

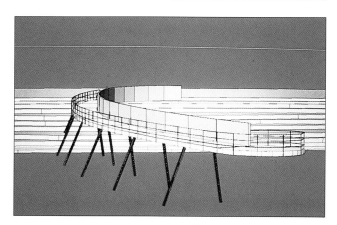

Will Alsop – Alsop and Störmer Architects,
ABOVE and CENTRE: Crossrail, Paddington Station, London;
BELOW: Barrage, Cardiff Bay

designed a floating fire-station by Lambeth, architecture which moves. I do not actually like this kind of architecture very much, but we did it none the less. An interesting point in the planning permission was that Lambeth, being the local authority in question, does not like the use of the colour silver. We had submitted a sample of the external cladding, the colour of which was called 'silver' by the manufacturer; I believed that having that particular colour was important so I simply changed the name to 'light grey' and sent the same sample back, which they then claimed was much better. This example shows just how absurd certain situations are with which we have to deal.

I am sorry you did not get a crossrail station at Paddington, Piers, because I think you would have done a marvellous job. This was a nice project for us because one can design below and above ground, connecting the whole lot. The whole point about this is making that connection directly from underground full-sized trains to the sky. We had to end up with a space that could achieve this transformation, so we designed a glass line fin which actually bursts through the ground. This was a wonderful opportunity to build something on the scale of a cathedral. It is considerably longer than a cathedral and a little bit narrower than a nave, but it is actually the same height as Cologne Cathedral – twenty-eight metres.

Sometimes what we do or what we are thinking about is informed by climate, as in the case of the Barrage. The whole point of the Barrage was that it should be conceived not as a barrage, but as a lake, a lake to transform this part of Cardiff. I enjoyed this project (which is now under construction) because it was more a landscape project than architecture.

Otto Shteidler, Jean Nouvel and I had an idea of designing a 'Euro Tower', a deliberate notion to make the city of Lille more complex. The Mayor, the managing director of EuroLille, and Rem Koolhaas thought that as the whole area was going to be extended, it was time to confuse it even more, and hence were wondering if I would open an office to participate in this debate. It is this participation that is important, and over the last five years Rem has worked simply by having lunch with the Mayor and the Managing Director of EuroLille at least once a month – whether they have anything to discuss or not. If people object to the idea of the city of objects, then this is another way of doing it, it is actually born out of conversation, born out of a group of architects with commitment – that was the whole point of being there.

One of the problems that many of the architects sitting around this table will have encountered is that you can win a competition, you can check it just to make sure that it is a very legitimate competition, and then you can discover that having won it you have no money. If the competition organisers had initially stated the lack of finances you may still have continued, but may have also considered the consequences slightly more seriously.

I have undertaken a study for the city of Melbourne in designing the Museum of Modern Art. Australians are forthright in stating their budgets, and make no pretences if the finances are not as hoped for. This creates a special response in the architect, forcing one to be more creative in many ways. I was given a huge site of 750m x 200m, and the first thing I did – because it does not cost very much – was to cover it in bright orange concrete with a three metre high wall around it for security (because that's what museums and art are about). You have actually signalled to the world that this is a place for art which is to come, and the only other thing which you have added is a car park – which is revenue – and a second hand car dealership. (It seems to me that Melbourne's second passion, after sun, is looking at second hand cars.) This revenue would allow art to be commissioned and fill up this space over a period of time, perhaps building one or two special facilities that become evident, and after fifty years you close them and there begins a marvellous exchange from a gallery into a museum. Fifty years later you do the same thing somewhere else – one of the great things about a city emptying out is that it leaves large chunks of space where this can be done. Of course the danger for the future for the city is that it becomes totally dead in the centre, filled with museums.

Lastly, just to demonstrate a very different response, we designed a museum for Arthur Boyd in the middle of nowhere, halfway between Sydney and Canberra. This is both a public park and a place for art in the future. A couple of small galleries have been designed to take on some of his work in a temporary exhibition, and the main intervention here has been the addition of nine extra rocks in the landscape. Each rock has a function, and of course the irony here is that the climate is so wonderful in mid-winter that a building is not even really necessary. There is the looking rock, where visitors look at one of the places that Arthur used to paint; the writing rock and so on. You become very involved in each of the rocks, allowing or changing the relationship between the person experiencing the rock in a singular manner and the landscape; so in this case you raise the level of the table so you do not look down on the landscape. In some cases only the stars or music rock – on which the top can be used for performances – are visible. The talking rock – the art of conversation – is important. The rock revolves once every hour. And the rocking rock for dancing is the last one.

Thank you.

Paul Finch

Given the different countries you have worked in, would you say that having worked in Marseilles you have noticed that they are not culturally conservative, or is it that they are culturally conservative but they take on architecture as a definite cultural matter? So even if they are conservative, at least they are approaching it in a slightly different way through what might happen here.

Will Alsop

That is a difficult question to answer, because I always stand on the premise that everyone is conservative, including yourself, and that it is a question of convincing both yourself and these other people that something else might be appropriate. The French are interested in architecture and have a fantastic history of buildings to prove it. We cannot deny that, and I think that is terribly important. Obviously Frank has some experience of the French attitude as well. I would have to say, though, that Marseilles is not France, it is Africa.

We are doing a new building for Reuters in Moscow, and it is interesting that the authorities in Moscow are often very aware, and you often have conservatism as a form of protection. They are very aware that because of their strange or difficult economic state, they are tending to attract what you might call the cowboys of the investment world, who will build rubbish. In Moscow they believe that they are happy to have any investment in the city and hence will put up with the rubbish. In order to protect themselves they have become incredibly conservative. We are working on breaking this resistance to introducing new styles which break up the consistency of form.

So things vary for different reasons, but certainly I would think that France is the place where you really feel they are giving architects *carte blanche* to explore new avenues.

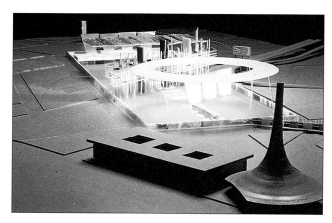

Will Alsop – Alsop and Störmer Architects,
ABOVE: Barrage, Cardiff Bay; CENTRE and BELOW: Museum of Modern
Art, Melbourne, Australia

Paul Finch

If I could perhaps have a comment on Berlin, we might bring Peter in on that for a view.

Will Alsop

I have already said all that I wanted to say on Berlin. It is somehow some sort of a lie, and I am disappointed by it to a certain extent, insofar as some of the most interesting architects in the world have carried out projects on Berlin, but only a few have been given the opportunity to implement them. Berlin could be the most extraordinary city in the world architecturally speaking, and yet it is not. I rather like Christoph Langhof, but there is a housing project by him which is an absolute dog, I would go bananas if I was living there, as grey colour seems to bring out the worst. It is enough to drive one to suicide, but it is environmentally friendly and that is the danger nowadays. As long as an architect has all these handles, he can sell projects because they are environmentally responsible, contextual, economic and so on. However, this architecture starts to fall into the idea of being a one liner rather than a series of very complex concept. If the soup is stirred correctly, they could work together.

Paul Finch

And do you agree with Jeff Kipnis' proposition that architecture must be transformational, or should be transformational, should make an attempt to be transformational? Is that what you feel is not happening in Berlin at the moment?

Will Alsop

I think we all respond to things. We reflect on what society wants or would allow, I suppose. Anyway, our job is to poke at those edges and to see really what they would allow, and you cannot go beyond that. I do not think there is a single building that has changed the world; I am sure Jeff will argue otherwise, but I maintain that a traffic engineer is more powerful and has a more dramatic effect on the architectural world around us, in terms of change.

Peter Cook

I believe we have been talking about individuality, creative mavericks, cultural conservatism and England. Occasionally I think that people like Will, myself, and our friends are treated as somewhat useful but costly, and occasionally we have built more on the strength – well, Will has, but on the whole we do not – and it is very funny when we go into Europe. The danger is to play it as the funny, eccentric Englishman. The late Warren Short used to say, apropos of American second or third rate architecture schools, that there was always an old Englishman and an old German, but they were always people you never knew of from both countries.

I think the reason I have always felt comfortable in LA is that, like London, you can get completely lost in it with the constant possibility that there is something interesting just around the corner. The danger of the acceptable tradition of the English eccentric is that he is alright as long as he does not have any real power. As soon as this breed comes close to having power, they are kept in their place.

I think there is also the positive aspect of being an off-shore island, which I believe links us with Japan in a curious way. We derive our main philosophical traits from mainland Europe, but we choose to have a low threshold of boredom, just as we do when we adopt philosophical traits from the US: our very happy low threshold of boredom allows us to keep half an ear open to them and still go back to the potting shed and get on with it. I find Japan is very similar, in that it obviously inherited much from China but deliberately chose not to play it correctly. I do not share Frank's enthusiasm for making a big issue of localism, but I think the edges are always very interesting because there they are like sort of cultural potting sheds – like Iceland or Grasse, as opposed to Vienna and so on. They are always places in which you can get away with strange things, as long as you have a couple of cronies. I think there are certain cities at certain times which provide sufficient numbers of like-minded people for one to escape the battering – whether the batterings are to do with lack of work, money, or of anybody who is interested.

At the moment, England, I think, has this problem. We still have a reasonably good airport and a fair number of places to publish, and I am surrounded by people who are not rushing to word processors, but there is a sort of danger. I think it is more possible for the third rate British building to be published than the first rate Argentinian or Vietnamese building. I am not sure whether that does a lot of good, because at the moment I think it would be quite correct to say that we are quite a minor architectural country. We are extremely provincial – if you look at the sort of work that is coming

through, very little of it will hold. I always use places that know, like Frankfurt: if you look at their cafés, they are on average better designed than cafés in London or if you look at some housing schemes and so on – whatever anyone measures architecture by. If we are absolutely honest, taking population by population, we have sunk some distance back. I do not think it is going to stay like that, I think the young are as nutty as fruitcakes – our current students are probably the nuttiest that I have seen in about ten years.

Archigram had its 450,000th exhibition not in London, New York, or LA, but in Vienna. Vienna is extraordinary: at the same time as our exhibition, there was a very, very good Le Corbusier exhibition; a gallery had just opened up a branch from Berlin; an exhibition of Fascist cities was being held in another building and there was also a Russian exhibition. That is a sum of five architectural exhibitions in a town of just 1.5 million. Vienna is still a conservative city (although they had just brought in Michael Sorkin as a Professor and I believe Dr Alsop is about to be given his chain of office) but it does make you think that London is a city which is conservatively fertile. Therefore we should have twenty exhibitions, sixteen such professorial roles and so on, but we do not. I do not like to be a grumbler but I do think we have the best nutters. It is how you market them, and our tradition is not to market them.

LA still has the very best nutter of the lot, and what are you doing Frank? I hate to think! I remember you saying that you grew up saluting the Queen as a Canadian boy scout! There are more very good second rate buildings in Vancouver than almost anywhere else I have been to, and that is another issue: whether you measure a city on three brilliant things if you can find them, or on the upper level of the second rate – in the same way in which you can measure architects.

Charles Jencks

I was struck by Will Alsop's presentation, as it seemed to be an approach not unlike Frank's. There is the same motivation of using artistic thinking as a weapon with which to break the log jam. What I would like to put forward is a position concerning this afternoon's subject: of individual imagination and cultural conservatism, and comment on what Will said about lying. He mentioned lying in the sense that we do not recognise the way the discourse is structured differently by society and by architects – the last Utopian profession. Architects are

the last profession which really does think what the city might be in an idealistic sense. This constantly puts us in a double bind. When Frank Gehry put forward the plan for the Disney Hall, a good architectural critic wrote in the LA times that 'this is a most important building on a prime cultural site; you have to support it, Frank is having trouble with it. It really will pull together the chaotic downtown culture with its riots and all that'. Somehow, in some way which was never quite explained, it was supposed to integrate fourteen major minorities – Hispanics right next door to Blacks and so on. Now, can architecture do that? Can it integrate a fragmented culture? No, of course it cannot, we have known that for a long time.

Let me illustrate the three main relationships between individual imagination and cultural conservatism. First is the *no-win situation*, the individual and cultural conservatism trade-off situation. If you get more of one side you get less of the other, or more of Prince Charles and a lot less of Piers Gough and Will Alsop. We are fooling ourselves if we do not think there is a trade-off. The second is a *negative-win situation* where everybody loses, and I think that is the one that Britain has been in for some time. This is the situation where the cultural conservatives say, 'right, these are the building codes, this is how it's going to be'. In effect it is the Leon Krier view of Europe, but he does not get the jobs or control it – nor even Quinlan Terry. Rather third-hand versions of tradition, which does not please either the traditionalists or the individuals. The last situation is the *positive-sum game*, a so-called 'win-win situation'. The obvious example of this is Florence in the Renaissance with its 45,000 citizens; 45,000 people created a situation where there was incredible individuality, and tradition. After the Second World War, Japan was a society with a strong holistic feeling and yet one where individuals flourished. That is what we want; a situation where there is *more* tradition, *more* individual creativity, and *more* pluralism.

That brings me to the present, and since 1986, the exhibition of Jim Stirling, Norman Foster and Richard Rogers, all of whom were subsequently knighted. The evening discussion at the Royal Academy, run by Jocelyn Stevens was depressing because he asked, 'why do the British not recognise their talent?' It was a sad evening and we all went away with our heads bowed. But look what has happened in the past five years! Two of them have become world-leading architects; High-Tech has emerged as *the* dominant style, and we no longer have the 1980s three-way battle between Modernism, Post-Modernism and Classicism. Two things have happened in the 1990s: there is a new kind of dominant which is more pluralistic and tolerant, and secondly (this was what I really wanted to discuss) there has been a shift in how discourse works now. Suddenly even the Prince realises it is no longer a matter of ideology; he has also become pluralistic. And leaders have emerged who believe in the pleasure of architecture. For example, Will Alsop, Rem Koolhaas, Zaha Hadid, Alessandro Mendini, Nigel Coates, Jean Nouvel, Philip Starck, Peter Eisenman and Arata Isozaki, and the fifteen who always appear on the short lists. Ideology has become only a pretext, and we are moving into new territory where people like Gehry are the major force. It is hard to put a word on this. Frank forces us to *accept* the text when he appears on the cover of *Time* magazine. We are getting a global culture which is not ideological; for the first time since the Rococo an architecture of pleasure that dares declare itself. This is a force in itself, and that is a funny situation because we do not know how we respond as professionals. We do not have any discourse in which we can say this creativity and pleasure are better than that. Instead of hiding behind function, cost and High-Tech, we are finally admitting, as a profession, that it is our responsibility to defend architecture as a creative art.

Adam Carouso

We obviously live in a world that is pluralistic. You are making a link between the work of Will Alsop and Frank Gehry, but I have great difficulty in making that connection in such a quick way. You insistently refuse to justify why things are the way they are. But everything is the way it is for a reason, and the sort of architecture that I am interested in and have been trying my hardest to do, is an architecture which is *far more conceptual* and does not have to do with a kind of a self-directed formalism. What I find so inspiring about Gehry's architecture is that it is engaging in a profound way with where it is coming from, both within a political and physical context. I would like to point out from that work the use that Gehry makes of certain Post-Modernist conceptual sculptors or artists who have worked with those concepts. They inform the way Gehry's buildings respond and come out of their context.

Something was mentioned earlier about highway engineering and motorways: Rem Koolhaas has a huge enthusiasm for motorways and takes people on drives

on flyovers because they are so amazing and poetically exciting. I think we can do a lot better than just say they are there. They are powerful, they do govern the way we use the cities, they have direct consequences on political decisions, making them more direct than architecture often is. But if you look at what Koolhaas has done at Lille, more or less successfully, he says there are all these roads, all these systems of infrastructure, and there is a certain amount that he as the architect or planner or whatever, can do to just massage these lines of infrastructure. Some of them are existing, some are proposed, and he just moved them a little bit so that they actually started to relate to each other; started to engage and make a context into which more conventional ideas of architecture can be placed.

That seems to be the place where architecture has to go – it has to engage these things which we have not engaged with in the past. We have to move away from the idea of relating to a conventional architectural history. What is avant-garde is to look at a motorway and a situation and to do the little bit that you are allowed to do as an architect, and actually articulate the situation as being potentially rich and beautiful – exactly what Richard Serra's 'Tilted Ark' was attempting to do. That sculpture was never trying to be polite or nuts – it was meant to be belligerent, and that is why the security guards in the federal building found it offensive. It has a security risk as people could hide behind it.

Paul Finch

The points you raise are interesting. Will's work in Cardiff on the Barrage was involved at a very early stage with the engineers, and this relationship between an architectural project and a straight engineering project is increasingly cropping up in Britain. For example, redesigning every bridge on every motorway in Britain is being undertaken, because a lot of the concrete bridges are corroding, which makes the British Steel Corporation very happy. Hence, this is not just a theoretical area.

Adam Carouso

But it is not interesting at that level, as architects are being co-opted to put a rubber stamp on everything.

Tony Fretton

The issue centres around the forces which direct and influence society in say, highways. Highways have a very specific set of priorities – they create individual

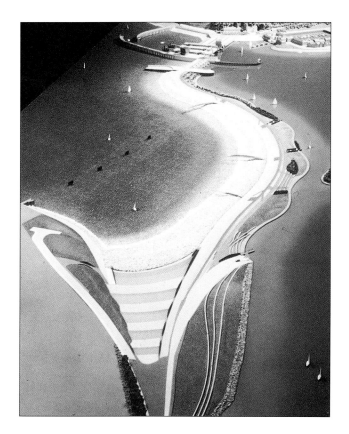

transportation to distributed suburbs, a picture with which European architects are deeply uncomfortable. I think architects have to recognise their distance from the sources of power, and also their distance from the centres of aesthetic existence. I was uncomfortable with this, with the ideas that have been promoted, and that just drives me back to the view that an architect engages his critic and constitutes a timely part of the production of the city. I think architecture's role is to actually mirror the reconstitution of the intelligentsia in society which has become marginalised.

Charles Jencks

The danger of Carouso's position is that it marginalises the architect to Edge City and leaves the centre to Prince Charles and traditionalists. But, in any case, I bet at the end of the day, we will all be *de facto* pluralists; that is to say we will not defend any one position solo. In the 1980s Prince Charles emphatically put forward a monothematic answer, and then we had a whole lot of Ayatollahs. But now with the pleasure of architecture we are more content with developing difference.

Adam Carouso

Can I just make one small response? Regarding those traditional city centres which you have described, Charles, I think it is a case of how we imagine it, and the regard in which we hold it varies from age to age, along with our historicising and our fictionalisation. So I would argue that the forces which you are trying to relegate to the suburbs are actually active in the centre of the city. Frank interests me because he recognises that. Pete, you actually relegate English artists to the role that is prescribed to them – which is by acting in the right way. What is very interesting about Roger is that his work is surrounded by very acute comments and interesting writers. I am just going to deviate slightly: writers today place emphasis on architecture re-theorising itself, and believe that the interesting architects are those who build and think. It interests me, Will, that you do not feel the need to advance the argument which surrounds your work, but you *do* require intelligence in those viewing it.

Will Alsop

That *assumes* that there has to be intelligence in the way one views work. What I am trying to avoid is a prescription, exactly some of the things you described. You are advocating a prescription for how I might make

Will Alsop – Alsop and Störmer Architects, Barrage, Cardiff Bay

it work or what my response should be to what I perceive as happening in the world. Therefore I am not sure what, in your view, I should be doing or indeed, what *you* should be doing to make it a better work.

Chris McCarthy

I have been working with architects as an engineer from Arup, and it is my honest belief that Will's work fits in with the landscape as much as these helium balloons floating along the Royal Academy ceiling. I think that one is sometimes taken too seriously but, putting the view of the engineer forward, the engineer's conservative definition is: the maximum use of materials, skills and energy for the benefit of mankind. But now we are in to the conservation of the future of the human race, and we talk about sustainability, sustainability for future generations which do not even exist. I think that is extremely difficult. We often view our work by the system that exists today, yet we are building for people of the future, so as engineers we are looking for an architect or individual who has skills in predicting the behaviour of future generations in their built environment.

It is like virtual reality, because it creates wealth and suspension and experimentation, which leads to a technical revolution. However, from my study of history we should expect the acceptance of our work for future clients from the existing system with great dishonesty. Piers' comment about being disappointed at winning five out of six competitions is a very important point, because we cannot expect our work to be accepted by existing systems and often it is under question but, unlike our predecessors, when working with technology it is very much more difficult to predict the future, the interaction of people with our built environment, our virtual reality environment – and I think that is why we are here today. I think the understanding of the future behaviour of individuals which Will was talking about – the drug takers and the non-drug takers – is the problem. On the other hand, is it really worth the effort, because we do not receive immediate acknowledgement for our talents? I think that is the problem of the design process. We can no longer look at history for guidance. We are faced with a great and difficult task, as it is impossible to predict the future of the nation – not in hundreds of years, or in tens of years, or even in five minutes. I think the focus should be more on the argument of what we have done and what we are doing,

that is more on trying to define making use of the people that are here today to help us understand the future and the people it will contain.

Frank Gehry

I have never before been honoured with the amount of respect and kind words which have been said about me today, from a group of architects this size. Hey Charlie, maybe I can get knighted!!

There are a lot of micro-climates of talent in architecture and language and this situation is similar throughout the world. I think a pluralistic society requires *all* of us to survive, to grow and prosper and realise our talents to the highest and best use, and to help others achieve the same, because we need more help and more talent. There is a lot of talent which does not *get* through the system. As a teacher you are *very* aware of that. People are being cut off from the past, and there are always more possibilities for expansion throughout the world. Most of us believe in democracy, but the system has created a world that looks strange, chaotic and different, and we do not like it. We are struggling and it is easier to go back to models which are more coherent and seem more seductive now. We have to remember that those models came under a different political time and philosophy. If we are to survive, we need to live in the present and try to work towards the future. I will reiterate what I have said many times: I cannot face my children if I tell them I have no more ideas and I have to copy something that happened before. It is like giving up and telling them there is no future for them.

The work that interests me now is to do with collaboration, about developing relationships with other talents and surviving with one's ego intact; with speaking one's own language and having one's own firm beliefs and ideas within the context of a collaboration. I think that Rem's work in Lille sounds like that kind of effort. I have not seen it, but if I were to push anything that is what I would work towards. I have tried to do it with other architects, sometimes successfully, and sometimes not, but in the years I have left, that is what I want to do. I want to work with groups of people developing building complexes, developing not a unilateral decision about what the city should be – I do not trust my own judgement in such a context – but how to survive and how to make identifiable pieces of the buildings which are coherent with others, creating a

Will Alsop – Alsop and Störmer Architects, ABOVE and OPPOSITE: L'Hôtel du Département, Marseilles, France

democratic (whatever that is) model for our world. I do not like the responsibility of having the world put upon my shoulders – to solve everything in one building. I cannot accept that position, I am not capable of doing it.

Max Hutchinson

Two things if I may: firstly, we have celebrated eccentricity this afternoon on many occasions – the beautiful mind of the eccentric English. It is a pity we have not mentioned our fear, our terror of the *avant-garde*. We are so frightened of it, we have not even got an English name for it, and it frightens me that despite the fact that at Oxbridge, for example, where we have some of the most *avant-garde* thinking in science, philosophy, the arts and literature, the dons are commissioning some of the most tedious and conservative buildings imaginable.

The second point I would like to make is that Will said that he was not going to talk about the process, which I think is a great shame. There was a dreadfully desiccated, anally-retentive exhibition at the RIBA last year on the art of the process, with white tables filled with pencils and sheets of paper; but Will's was at a dinner table and I wanted to know how this man creates his buildings. I think elucidation of the processes that Frank, Piers or Will go through is essential in the consideration of these issues – more particularly so the way in which those processes reflect on education.

It is a shame there are not more young people in this room today and that more young people do not come to these meetings. I go around most of the schools of architecture in this country every year, and find that the teaching methodology has not changed since I was a student. Most of the schemes are the same; if we really want to try and make some impact with the conversations we have had in this room today, that is where we have to start

Robert Maxwell

I am sorry there are opinions still to be aired – for me this has been one of the most interesting debates Academy Group and The Royal Academy have set up, because it actually continues the main philosophical problem I have tried to grapple with in my writings: the whole process by which society transforms itself over time. It is natural that younger architects would see the situation as unnaturally stable. No doubt, to the sperm the egg appears to be unconquerable. An unsuitable

metaphor, but people who are being successful at the moment (and I include Piers, Frank and Will) are enjoying the power of being able to just do it. Thus, all have the same thing, an enormous self-confidence in their own processes. What if they gave it away? Why should it become institutionalised? It is their secret, their power, and I think that is exactly what makes a person creative. It is all down to this incredible self-confidence.

Will said some very interesting things to the effect that he has to balance out not only the clients but himself, to know what he will do. I think that is very significant, because I think that every individual needs to balance the risks. I have pondered on this amateur psychology for years, but do not know how much it is true. The fact is that I can take on new things better at some times than at others, and take on board new things only when I feel pretty secure about my system. However, when I feel under threat I find it more difficult to cope with new things. There is a sense in which we all exist in a kind of continuum of security and insecurity. The less our intolerance and the higher our security, the more we are prepared to let a more variable order take over. Perhaps it is more a stretch between order and variety.

The traditional way is comforting – you have lines, you can make small extensions of the system. But when you are really very confident with yourself you can make quite big decisions in a system, and even make a new system work. The transformation which Goerg Simmel identifies is one where we do not know where we are or what our thinking is until it is made visible to us through our forms; forms are therefore an essential means of bringing out our potential and showing us where we are and what we can do. The minute a new form comes out and is accepted, it becomes an obstacle and has to be fought against, in turn. This is not just a generational thing, it is a cultural thing, to do with individual psychology and we are thankful for these bright people and their enormous self-confidence.

Paul Finch

It only remains for me to thank The Royal Academy and Mary Anne Stevens for allowing the Academy Forum to hold this event. I would also like to thank Academy Group and VCH for their generous sponsorship in making this possible. We did have a possible working title at one stage for this event, when we were all considering how one describes Frank Gehry's work. The best headline we could think of was 'Form Swallows

Function', but then I did see a rather good headline the other day about Gehry, 'Skating On Thick Ice', both of which I find enjoyable. I think we have had an interesting discussion with a rather more complicated title than we chose, and I would very much like to thank Piers and Will for agreeing to give presentations. I was interested to hear from Piers, that at one stage he was interested in being either Baroque or Mannerist, but ended up as Baroque around the clock – the clock in Westbourne Grove. For Will, I suppose his theme might be 'little white lies', in respect to the relationship between the architect, the planner and the client, which gives architects their power, the occasion to perform their magic, their fees, and what I would like to describe

as the wages of synthesis. I suppose the proof of the British pudding is the appointment of the architects who are going to do the only really substantial new part of Windsor Castle. They are the architects who rebuilt the grand buildings on a processional route quite close to Jeff Kipnis' favourite London venue, where they perform the Trooping of the Colour once a year. On that note I would like to say how relieved I am to hear that Frank Gehry is modest enough not to accept the burden which Jeff would like to impose on his shoulders: to pretend that it is either desirable or appropriate for the architect, through the single building, to imagine, at least temporarily, that it is a good thing if architects, alone, rule the world.

Frank Gehry

'Since I'm so Democratic I accept Conformists'

A Lecture on Recent Work

Philip Dowson

A warm welcome to you all here at the Academy, and a particularly warm welcome to Frank Gehry for coming to address us. This is the Fourth Annual Academy Lecture to be sponsored by the Academy Group and to be held at the Royal Academy. It is part of the whole programme the Royal Academy is engaging in as part of a wider view of what we believe we *should* be doing. It is also a great pleasure for us to be able to continue this collaboration with the Academy Group. The influence of Southern California speaks for itself, and so it is marvellous to have Frank Gehry with us to speak of his own unique and distinguished work, where perhaps suggestion, an evocation, seems to have a greater significance than statement and position. Charles Jencks called Gehry 'the first Deconstructionist'.

Charles Jencks

Thank you Philip. Thank you all for coming. I am happy to be here. I am an old friend of Frank's, having known him for twenty-two years. As I count myself amongst his friends, I would like to say something about him in this capacity. First, his incredible generosity: Philip Johnson gives a lot of young architects jobs and when Frank was in trouble, Philip gave him work and recognition. Frank has carried on that tradition, and it is important to see generosity in a profession which is highly competitive. I can think of few other architects who have this spirit. Richard Rogers, in this country, is one. Secondly, unlike so many other competitive architects and Charles Moore (who was a good friend of ours), Frank is not a macho architect – nor do I want to say he is a hermaphroditic architect. Architecturally speaking, he is not sexually gendered and that brings a refreshing aspect to his work. Thirdly, Frank was incredibly kind to my family and myself when we were ill. Fourthly, he is a nice guy. I know 'nice guys don't win wars', and I know that to say

'he is a nice guy', is almost a form of abuse. In some circles it is said, 'nice guys apparently do not make good architects', because of course they have to fight for what they believe in. Since Darwin's day we have heard that nice guys do not win wars, but apparently Post-Darwinism is now saying otherwise.

I will spare you this new theory and a few anecdotes that have developed over the past twenty-two years, such as the fact that when we first met we went on a boat trip and he gave me some marijuana. Being in America during the Clinton generation, we did not inhale. That was the point. And I tried to kill him once, by accident, but he will probably tell you about that!

I want to focus on one specific idea: 'Gehry as a great architect'; perhaps the Picasso of architecture or maybe the Hockney of architecture, because of his imagination and the way his creativity constantly leads into new territory. Like Picasso he makes us follow him into the unknown, picking up one new idea after another and then developing it. I would like to mention four of these new ideas. Firstly, the perspectival space evident in the Davies House of 1972. This was for the painter Ron Davies who, as it happened, was also doing skewed perspectival paintings. This led to the tradition of anamorphic perspective, which is most developed in the work of Zaha Hadid. Secondly, the use of cheap, *demodé* materials in a creative way, such as wood studs, chain link, corrugated metal and a whole series of throwaway elements. This has rescued them from banality, encouraging us to see them in a new light and understand parts of our environment, which people like Picasso made apparent to us through creativity. Thirdly, the invention of small-block planning, which Leon Krier and Jane Jacobs also adopted. They pointed out its social and urbanistic importance in the 60s and late 70s. Frank added to this small-block planning by discovering that a convivial city could be made of juxtaposed pavilions of *one-room* buildings. Lastly, the personal search into a new language of curved forms which are not quite Baroque, Rococo, Art Nouveau or Expressionist – as previous research into curved forms has been. But they certainly come from nature, and are close to the lessons of chaos theory and complexity theories. These are right at the cutting edge of science *and* architecture.

I could go on, but the point is that such creativity is at once political and spiritual. It is political because it has the power to lead through many exciting, dangerous, unknown and sexy avenues. Invention is always attractive because it appeals to the mind; Raquel Welch once said that the brain is the sexiest organ of the human body. Creativity is attractive and political because we are curious as a human species; and as an animal we want to learn to adapt to a changing universe. This potency to invent has to be perceived by an audience.

This creativity in action is also spiritual because it shows the presence of *cosmogenesis* – evolution in action. It was a point known to a previous generation of artists at the beginning of this century, especially Kandinsky and early founders of the Bauhaus. Kandinsky explored this theory in depth in *The Spiritual in Art*, and for the last seventy years this notion of spirituality as creativity in action has been suppressed by a secularised Modernism. Frank's work shows, I believe, what would have happened, if in 1921 at the Bauhaus and throughout Europe and America, this tradition had not been suppressed.

Frank Gehry

I am happy to be here, even though I was compromised into coming! Charlie was lying in his bed in LA, very ill, and took advantage of the situation (he always works as you know, even when he is ill) and made me promise to come to this talk. You know how you agree to things six months or so in advance, and then wish you had said 'no'? I have two kids who I am trying to get through high school, and it is driving me nuts, so I want to go home! I am a do-it-yourself father. I will not malign Prince Charles tonight as I have been quoted as doing. I was raised in Canada, and I used to stand up for the national anthem – 'God Save The King' as it was then – and I proved the last time I was here that I can still sing, 'There'll always be an England'. If you need verification of my ancestry I will sing it!

The last time I spoke in the presence of Robert Maxwell was at Princeton, and at the end of my talk he raised his hand in the question period and said: 'Mr Gehry, do you have nightmares? How do you concoct that stuff?' We were in a symposium, and during its duration he had a transformation of opinion and came up to me afterwards and very sweetly apologised. I cherished that.

The chain-link stuff was about denial, I was always fascinated by denial. I have never lain on the couch in a shrink's office – I have just had a guy talk to me a lot. But the idea that when somebody decided to use a material which was being produced and used worldwide and made everybody mad, made me interested enough to pursue it. I did so, as I have done with several ideas in my life, and I think I still push at that area.

Charlie helped me concoct the title of this talk, 'Since I am a democrat . . . ' The context of an earlier symposium was about the issue of creativity in London, Europe and America, and specifically, what the role of it is in a democratic world. For me LA has been in the front line of that kind of chaotic product of democracy. We do not have any historical architecture to ground us or hold us – I will not say hold us back, because I do not think it needs to hold you back. LA is a pretty messy town built on the automobile and on freewheeling democracy, where everybody has their own rights and the architecture and the buildings reflect this.

When you get on the train of the future, out of architectural school, you get on with a certain *gestalt* around you. I began in the post-war era when decoration was bad and functionalism was good, and I held on to values such as planning and saving the world. I found that these ideas that I came on the train with, were constantly being challenged by some young kid who got on a later train, with another set of values. Because they got on later, they are on a higher moral plane. The models for me were Frank Lloyd Wright, Le Corbusier, Mies Van der Rohe and Alvar Aalto (Aalto was my favourite at that time). If there were only half a dozen models in the early 5Os, there are well over one hundred high-powered architects with high recognition practising around the world today. But the higher moral plane is now questioning all this, questioning the whereabouts of social responsibility. I am going to start tonight's talk with social housing in Germany, just to prove that I am socially responsible.

I believed that just becoming an architect was an act of social responsibility; when I got out of school with a planning background, I did not want to do rich guys' houses, I only wanted to work on big plans. There were not very many around and they certainly did not want to hire characters like us, so I dealt with what I got, and I soon got what I deserved and that was that. I accepted my lot optimistically and worked with what I had, making it what I chose to make it, and in that context the *process* became very important to me. I was interested in what the artists were doing, how they were working with materials and craft, and consequently learnt a lot from them. I wanted to deal with the craft, I wanted to deal with the people who were *making* the buildings, I wanted to engage them – which is not the way we are trained as architects. I wanted to break down those barriers – which will take two more lifetimes. But I made relationships with the Sheet Metal Workers' Union of the World a few years ago, did an exhibit for them, and shook hands on a deal that they would help me with technical assistance wherever I went. They have lived up to it, even in Bilbao, Spain. They have helped me to work within my budget, have stuck to their guns and have made possible some of my successes in the use of those materials.

I am a *slow* architect, I take a long time to create, so the thought that my building ideas are just tossed in the air and land is the furthest thing from the truth. The day after the earthquake in LA, a reporter from New York asked me if I wasn't happier now that LA looked more like the rest of my work. I told him that I was pleased that God finally saw it my way. The process has led me to the craziest thing I have ever been involved with, and that is the computer. When I started out I speculated then that somewhere along the line I would fall out with whatever is happening. I often wondered where it would be and in the last years I have found it to be the computer! I am computer-illiterate: I do not know how to turn it on, I am scared of the thing. My office is now filled with them and I will not walk into the room where they are because I fantasise they are going to swallow me – but I will talk about that with the buildings.

Architecture is not a unilateral project. It needs clients and people who have desires and needs, and I have found that the best buildings for me are when I engage the client. In order to work with them I have to explain myself as the project develops, so that it is not hocus pocus. I talk them through the models and drawings, and try to tell them what my purposes are. I find that the straighter I am about that, the more likely I am to succeed in achieving a building that they and I like. The market-place, of course, edits us all out – which we were talking about earlier in the symposium: why better architects are not better received, especially in their home town. Just as there are so many extraordinary architects in London who fail to receive commissions, there are so many who are in the same dilemma in LA; it is the same everywhere. My name was put up for a courthouse, and the General Services Administration that runs the government buildings just laughed at the idea. In America the President of the United States probably does not know anything about architecture, they have tended not to over the years. It is nice to visit France where the government is involved, and even here in Britain there is more involvement. Even though I do not agree with some of the Prince's ideas, he is aware and involved, and that is positive.

PAGE 38: American Center, Paris, France, 1988/91-93

Recent Work

The programme for social housing in Frankfurt, where I have worked, is beyond belief. I think this is due to the planning director Dr Lynn and the people from the Green Movement. Government agencies have brought in a number of architects from all over the world. Peter Eisenman is doing something and so is Fumihiko Maki. We were given a small piece of land near the airport in Frankfurt, and the project centres around connecting the greenbelts. There is a train and a school and all the civilised things that should be around for housing. Somehow they have got it all right on a very tight budget. I took one of the buildings and created a landscape site, on which I set one of the buildings like the main player on a stage. I then gave it more presence and added some corner buildings made of brick, which gave them the appearance of having been there longer.

The University of Iowa commissioned me to build a laser laboratory – the metallic part houses the offices, the stone part the laser labs – and then there is the sculptural piece which I did wrong, with the consequence that it looks like a fish or a boat. This section houses the support labs which, because of the programme, are windowless. The laser block has a pipe canyon in it, into which I dumped all the pipes which would normally have come into the roof; hence I was able to take advantage of the opportunity to create a sculptural piece in front of the building and make it out of copper, relating it to the copper of the Student Union. The other side of the building is built of metal and crystal and relates to the power station further up river. I must admit that I have never been to see this building. The people who I worked with on this building disappeared, evaporated into the university system. The purpose for the building then changed, and it no longer held any interest for me to go there.

FROM ABOVE: Social Housing, Frankfurt; Iowa Advanced Technology, Laboratories Building, University of Iowa, Iowa City, Iowa 1987/89-92

There is an art school in Toledo, Ohio, which relates to an art museum. This is in a long, three-pedimented, white marble building from the nineteenth century. The Museum Art School was originally housed in the basement of this building, but when the museum had to expand, it was decided to build the school elsewhere, as it could not be built it in the same style. The problem was whether the students would lose their direct contact with the museum as, on finishing school at the end of the day, the chances were that they would get into their cars and go home. Hence, the client stressed the importance of connecting the two, while keeping the existing structure intact. My idea was to compress the programme as tightly as possible. This would negate the expansive movement of the museum, making it compact almost to the point of a visual explosion.

Architects who have been practising some time know that we are all asked to design bird houses, dog houses, and whatever else you can imagine for various charities. The city of Hanover asked ten architects to design bus stops; this was one of the first of those things I have ever accepted because it looked reasonable. My bus stop is made of green and white (the colours of the bus company) in stainless steel. I believe the stainless steel was made in Britain.

One of the largest campuses in the United States, the University of Minnesota in Minneapolis, contracted me to build a new art museum. The original museum had been in an old classical building, buried and inaccessible. As Minneapolis is famous for its Museum of Modern Art, enjoying extensive patronage and awareness (next to New York it is probably one of the most important art cities in the US), the university was keen to share Minneapolis' cultural glory, so it thought to benefit further cultural awareness by building a kunsthalle place to show artefacts which could not be shown in other museums for whatever reasons. The tallest room in the existing Walker Art Center of Minneapolis was seventeen feet high, but we wanted space which would allow for bigger works, for pieces which could not be shown elsewhere. As this venture was to become an art partnership between the university

FROM ABOVE: Art school, University of Toledo, Ohio 1990/91-92; Bus stop, Hanover, Germany; University of Minnesota Art and Teaching Museum, Minneapolis, Minnesota, 1990/91-93

and the city, the new building had to be impressive and worthy of its contents. The facade started as a corrugation because both the offices and the foyer were to face up river, down river and straight ahead. So I started with a corrugation and then deformed it from there so that the relationship to the campus is defined. I initially worked with a stainless steel that was much more benign and shiny, but it soon became obvious that it would merge insignificantly into the grey weather of Minneapolis. The back of the building which faces the campus is in brick and it will remain thus temporarily, as fund-raising is being carried out at present for another gallery to be built, which will make the connection back to the university.

I have followed art and artists since I was young, but this was my first art museum from scratch. The galleries are rectangular. There is an enfilade of rooms along the diagonal, and the openings between the galleries have a skylight that hooks into a steel member which spans the room. Hence, none of the walls are supporting walls. This means that the room can be cleared to become one big room, which will of course change the natural light. Those of you who are involved in museums will know that natural light is going out fast and museum directors around the world are looking to five-foot candles and very low light levels to preserve works of paper and art, about which there is tremendous concern. The future of museums is changing. Light has to be controllable – both natural and artificial light. The skylights I designed for the Minneapolis Museum can be controlled by the push of a button, or they can be closed completely and five foot candles can then be used to throw subdued light upon the valuable artefacts.

The lighting systems I have always found too overpowering are track lights. I believe one needs a system that is not a system – if you have several systems, no one system in particular becomes the overbearing one. I chose to design an indirect cove with fluorescent lighting which bounces indirect light from the ceiling onto all the paintings in the room. It is a dull, flat light, so we added a mono point system which can highlight and add track if necessary. We then added a footlight which sits on the floor and can be used for works which do not have textural characteristics or do not look bad with reversed lights on.

One of the galleries in the Minnesota Art and Teaching Museum

The American Center, Paris, France, 1988/91-93

The American Center building in Paris has been very overexposed, because like a lot of cultural institutions today, it has had its difficulties with finances and there were problems regarding its opening. When I started this structure there were a lot of surrounding buildings which looked like Paris, and by the time the Center was completed, the surrounding context resembled social housing in Denmark. The landscape was a beautiful nineteenth century park, filled with warehouses and paving of weathered cobbles from that period; it was beautiful and poetic. All of that has been replaced with new cobbles and landscape architecture; so the park was turned into a building, mostly with steps which resemble those that lead up to a grand library.

I used to lived in France a long time ago. I like the stone of France and I like the roof tops. The American Center has a very complicated programme, including a theatre, an art museum, a language school, an art school, a restaurant, a bookstore, a travel agency, a department store, apartments, studios, two block box theatres, and much more, all plugged into the French zoning envelope. Because of the restricted space, the corner had been cut off. This tortured vision upset me for a year until I realised we could enter the building from the park side. However, the idea was to express all the energy of the building within a very tight budget: the reports in the press that this cost $40 million are not true. The hard costs for the building were $21 million, so it was not overly expensive.

Parisian stone is very effective as a stucco material; we have used it everywhere and it does not once look out of place. There was a lot of experimenting with the cascade of glass on the park side: that was the one-timer for all of us. How does one create window-walls which are so big but not overpowering? All the work on the building was carried out with a French architect as an associate, Roger Subbo, one of the best working relationships I have ever had. The French bureaucracy, which one of the architects was talking about earlier, is very well informed about architecture – unlike the United States where every time you mention the word architect, they run away. In France they treat the architect like a human being.

The interior of the building, the theatre, is multi-functional, but in designing the space, I asked the client to pick one use as having priority. Since he was an actor he picked legitimate theatre. The room can be used for music, and it opened the other night with David Byrne singing. I was reported in the London *Independent* as having designed constipated interiors and I think there is some truth in that. A lot of mixing and pushing was done to get as much into this one building as possible.

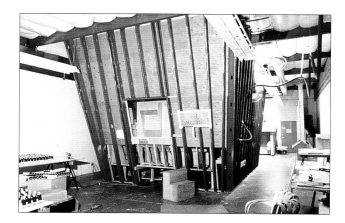

In Los Angeles I have been working on the Concert Hall, which is named the Walt Disney Concert Hall because the widow of Walt Disney donated the money (it has nothing to do with the company that built Euro Disney, although I suspect the latter received some of their funds from the same source). I won the competition, she liked the interiors of my building and told me that she had in mind a little thatched roof cottage for the exterior. We finally agreed that I could do the exterior as long as she could choose the interior design. We were guided in the competition – and Jim Stirling was one of the competitors – by an acoustical expert from France who led us to develop schemes with separate little spaces. However, when we won the competition we were told by several other experts that those arms had to be lobbed off. The Philharmonic chose a Japanese acoustician, Dr Nagada, who told me to do one thing, while Dr Kramer (who our client had brought in) suggested another. I finally decided to bring both men together in the same room and have them talk about it in front of me – and that was one of the wildest experiences in my life. They were extremely polite to one another, and each said the other was *the* greatest acoustician. Of course Dr Kramer, being German, was very feisty and got belligerent as the evening wore on while Dr Nagada, being Japanese, was very polite – so won by his politeness. However, it had been confusing to say the least. Our client liked the animation of the winning idea with the separate rooms, and asked us to try and capture that.

The final result was very similar to the Concertegebouw in Amsterdam, especially in proportion. The Concertegebouw has seven hundred seats behind the orchestra; we have three hundred. I think of it as a music barge, some kind of ship with a canopy which you can board to listen to music. The barge is made out of wood with flying sails, which works well visually, but in fact the material and the shapes are of acoustic importance. All the shapes were derived acoustically, with a little help from me, of course, and I am now fine tuning the negative space. I

The Walt Disney Concert Hall, Los Angeles, California, 1988/92-97
FROM ABOVE: Model; constructing the model

wanted the building to fly under one mast, under one aesthetic as it were, so I started to carry those shapes into the exterior. The problem arises when you show these forms to the contractor and say, 'we are going to build this concert hall within this budget'. They just laugh and send you packing before you have had a chance to show them how to build it. With the help of some friends in France – the people who make the Mirage fighter – we were able to analyse the stone shapes and stay within a budget of five per cent, using double-curve stone. We stuck within that budget, presented it to the contractors, and told them we were within the guidelines and had the software already worked out for the curved pieces of stone. One particular piece of stone was the most difficult, as it had to be cracked for the two shapes to come together. When you look at it you realise that it is fairly flat, with very little curve in each individual piece or the aggregate. Hence we were able to demystify into a simple language that the contractor could understand. This was the one piece of the building that came in on budget. The computer analysed the stone and from that we made a model, almost like a shop drawing, to be certain that the shapes were exactly to our specifications.

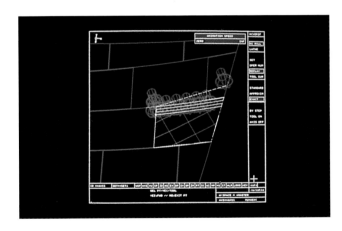

*The Walt Disney Concert Hall, Los Angeles, California, 1988/92-97
FROM ABOVE: computer-analysed and cut curve of the roof; computer cutting, derived from the French system of calculating the curves of aeroplane wings*

If you think London would be scared of me coming to do a building here, you can imagine what happened when I went to Prague. President Havel's grandfather designed a building which was so popular that many more were consequently built. Prague's nineteenth-century architecture is truly outstanding. In Prague we were invited to design a commercial office building for a Dutch company; it is tiny and will not be a big money-making project. Each floor is about five hundred square metres, so efficiency is not the highest priority, but the client wanted something that would fit its requirements, the city context and the textures – something which would solve the problems for the developer and would not copy the nineteenth-century architecture. Moreover, President Havel had to approve it. I presented the design to him, and, since the building was neighbouring his property, he had the right to veto it. His wife is a friend of Prince Charles and did not like it, but he did and his decision prevailed since he was the president.

In the time period I have been involved with Prague, three or four buildings in similar locations have been

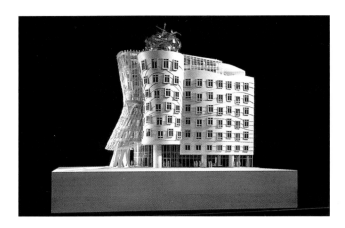

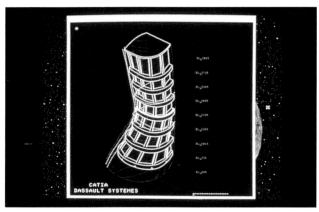

built along the river which are awful, yet nobody has complained in the public press or in the architecture school. Unlike the other buildings, mine had to go to a public referendum, and we ended up with 68 per cent of the voters pro the building. It has plaster, the windows jump up and down because the nineteenth-century buildings have floor heights which are not only different to ours but have windows at different levels. I only had from floor to ceiling to shift the window shape, so every other one touches the floor while the ones in between touch the ceiling. That is what gives it texture and works with the rest of the fabric of Prague. The street comes down and now goes straight into the river; by putting a bump there it directs the body language of the building towards the bridge. During the design process we exhibited many models and studies, but the press started to call the glass building Ginger and the tower Fred. They kept talking about Fred and Ginger and how Gehry's bringing Hollywood kitsch to Prague.

So they created what they wanted to see, and when I was speaking at the final presentation I explained that what they saw was purely in their imagination, in the eye of the beholder, and finished by telling them that they could call it whatever they liked. Sitting in the audience was a good friend of mine, Irving Lavin, from Princeton, an art historian of world renown, who said, 'You know architects don't know anything about what they're talking about. Gehry doesn't know, of course it's Fred and Ginger, of course they're here dancing on the banks of the river. They're not only dancing on the banks of the river, they're making love to Prague'. They loved it. So it is now Fred and Ginger.

I designed a museum for Vitra in Germany, and the owner asked me back to design his office building. His company manufacture and sell office furniture. There is a whole argument in the furniture world about where offices are evolving. Are they heading towards the virtual office? Office builders are always trying to invent some new idea because of real estate costs. They wanted to create a more efficient system with ideas which reminded me of an open office, so I worked on that concept. We explored various options and concluded that the interior should be fairly normal, as if it had curves and waves and so on. The clients would feel that the furniture looked good in the office, but would not fit

National-Nederlanden Office Building ('Fred and Ginger'), Prague, Czechosolovakia, 1993-95

in with their more normal homes. So the building started out with two rectilinear offices on either side of a villa construction, the entrance. This central section could afford to be more flamboyant and sculptural than the rest of the office. A conference centre and the wing covering it, and joining it to the main office building, was to be built as well. The articulated pieces are separate conference rooms. Once the recession is over, a smaller piece of parkland with another mother hen wing and building will be built. The relation of the office to the context is of paramount importance. A small office building is adjacent to the main building on one of the corners; hence, the box that shifts off the main box is making the relationship with that one. Across the road there is a three-storey house built of brick and wood, a factory and some villas strung along the street. Whatever success this building has is in relating to all those pieces and the freeway.

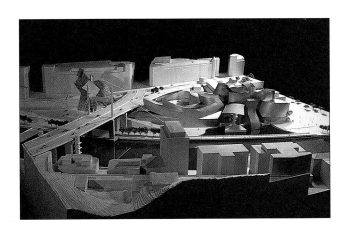

This building sits on the industrial waterfront of a tough city: Bilbao, in Spain. The competition was for a museum called the Guggenheim Museum – the last one was, of course, built by Frank Lloyd Wright in New York. For the competition we had the idea of a bridge bisecting the site, so that the city sits up on the ledge with the site below and further forward. The shapes facing the city are more blocky, imitating the city. One of the main streets comes directly into the site and a main public space; this directs people down to the river, so we decided to transform the river front into a cultural area. Ours is going to be the first building there. Thus you come in through the site, down a ramp and through a glass opening (and hung in that space, if I can figure out how to do it, will be a hologram of Frank Lloyd Wright looking disgusted with the whole thing). This space is not unlike Wright's at the Guggenheim which was not useable for art. That was a programmatic requirement in our case. The clients insist that living artists love to interact with that space, that it was provocative and engaging and so on, and that we would have plenty of room for the art and whatever was going to fill the rest of the building.

The images that inspired me, which every historian who talks about cities always focuses on, come from Fritz Lang's *Metropolis*. I thought that maybe I could create a similar vision, but create a modern space unlike those found in New York, where the buildings are so big

FROM ABOVE: New Headquarters for Vitra International, Ag, Basle, Switzerland, 1988/92-94; The Guggenheim Museum, Bilbao, Spain, 1993-97

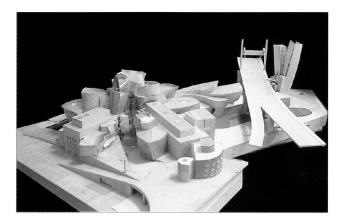

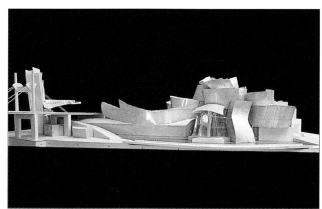

and overpowering that one cannot play the spaces. Ninety per cent of the galleries in this building are rectilinear.   In our office we tend to make three models before we start building: a small one, which is purely contextual; a bigger one to work out the shapes of the building and then a final interior model, which provides us with the opportunity to simultaneously develop shapes of the building and the interior. Hence I do not simply jam the interiors in at the end of whatever is left over.   Furthermore, we fit a tiny camera into the model from which we get polaroid shots to keep track of what we begin with, how we change ideas and so on. It is a good way of keeping a record of what we like, where we get lost, and so on. It is an elaborate process, and a part which resembles a dentist's drill is used to digitise the shapes into the computer and analyse them. Then a robot uses this information to make a model out of plastic. This takes a week and costs a tremendous amount, but it is like a shop drawing of the shapes completely replayed. The most exciting thing about this process is that we are able to control the costs of shapes on a big scale, and manage very tight budgets.

For what it is worth, I think the younger generation ought to consider becoming the master builders again, taking over the parental role in the construction process, instead of following the current fashion in America, where general contractors are part of the power structure of the city and have virtual control of the construction process, leaving the architect to play a childlike role. I think the tools mentioned earlier can reverse that process.

We entered the competition for a new museum in Berlin – but I shall not dwell on it for we came fourth. David Chipperfield came second, and I was very jealous because I wanted to be second. I did not want to *win* because the climate in Berlin is such that to win a competition like this would be a death sentence. Everyone would be out to get you and that is why I wanted to come second. The museum directors who have to work with contemporary demands are beside themselves. Masses of people are supposed to arrive and see the highlights in a couple of hours. I feel the museum world of the future is destined to be like that of the Louvre.

The Berlin competition was a proposal which dealt

The Guggenheim Museum, Bilbao, Spain, 1993-97

with urbanism and with the problem dealt with by Shinkel, of connecting all the parts of the city together. This is, in fact, very difficult. I tried to connect the building to the main road with an entrance in the Shtuler building which is in the middle of the design, and which has been rebuilt in the nineteenth-century style for some reason. The exhibits in this building are a sort of a pastiche on the nineteenth century, so now pastiche is going to be built on pastiche – an interesting idea.

Having already stated that I did not want to work on the private homes of the wealthy, I now have to admit that I am building a house for a single man in Cleveland, worth about $30 to 40 million. I did suggest that he should spend $5 million on the house and give the rest to charity. The house sits on the eighteenth hole of the fanciest golf club in Cleveland. When the man was a child he was thrown out of a pool on the same site for being a Jew, so he consequently bought all the land across the way. Philip Johnson designed the guest house and Claes Oldenburg, the sculpture. Maggie Jencks has been chosen to design a landscape sculpture. We started the project six years ago, so we are all somewhat weary. Social irrelevance gets me down but we are complying with the client's requests. We are attempting new ideas with glass and cast aluminium, and working with expensive techniques which we will probably never have the chance to work with again. It has been fun working with Philip, who is really quite brilliant. He has read everything, knows everything, has an encyclopaedic memory and tracks my thinking constantly when we are working together, often pre-empting my final move by a split second!

The Cleveland house may be socially irrelevant, but one project in particular which I was commissioned for had tremendous social relevance – a client asked us to design and build one hundred hockey rinks around the United States. There are many corporate organisations who are sponsoring the rinks which will be used by inner city kids who cannot afford to play ice hockey, and all the equipment will be provided. The children will have the opportunity to figure skate as well, and there will be a study centre with tutors so that the young can

FROM ABOVE: Competition entry for the Island Museum, Berlin, Germany; the Peter Lewis House, Cleveland, Ohio

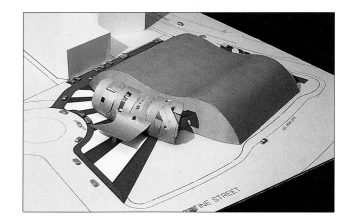

do their homework and be trained in the same place.

This hockey programme is the invention of none other than Michael Izenour who is the head of Disney. He used to play hockey as a child, so he and I have got together on this project.

In the future I would like to keep pursuing projects which have a real mix of ideas and people (including artists). In the past I have asked some of them to work with me and even though they like to take over, it is important to collaborate.

Robert Maxwell

I would like to apologise to Frank for referring to his nightmares; nightmares of course should be kept in private and never exposed. However, I have to say that I was not just being uncomplimentary, because I have always thought that nightmares are the more interesting parts of dreaming, and I am sure that in dreaming we are sometimes egged along to accept different things. I think Frank is one of these people who has learnt to accept different things, and we follow his lead. The critics and public in turn have to learn to accept different things, and this reminds me of my favourite poet (well before John Betjeman), Hillaire Belloc, with lines such as: 'Lord Lundy tried to mend the electric light himself, it struck him dead and serve him right. It is the business of the gentleman to give employment to the artisan'.

It is the business of the creative artist to give employment to the critic, and the critic's job is parasitical on the creative artist. The critic has to try and make sense of these wild forms and show that, after all, they are either not so odd or basically they correspond to the human animal. I hope that if Frank ever reads the crit which I wrote on the Vitra building, he will recognise that I saw in him a humanist – someone who extends our enjoyment.

It is supposed to be my job as this sort of last-words-person to give you some flavour of this afternoon's debate and of course, Frank's talk. Frank is a world figure, and we had the pleasure of sharing the day with two other figures from Britain who are fast becoming the same: Will Alsop and Piers Gough.

All three gave us three different versions of the work of the creative individual, and the debate tended to centre around the creative individual and cultural resistance. It is well known in the art world that when art

One of the 100 hockey rinks in the social programme which spans the United States

became too consumer-oriented and bourgeois during the nineteenth century, the avant-garde had to be invented in order to keep it moving well ahead of the bourgeoisie. We are now in the situation when many artists have to face the prospect and challenge of creating art that cannot be bought – this is interesting but difficult.

I think the most interesting aspect about Frank is that he does make art which can be bought and a lot of people *are* buying it. He has done his share of teaching. He works at making sure that the contractor will be able to build it (and that is something different from your off-the-cuff fellow in the bistro who gives you a sketch and asks you to work it out). Frank does real work, so I honour him as a professional, as well as an artist.

As to cultural resistance, our problem was to try and find out if other places – such as America – are more fortunate, in that the culture does not resist so hard, or whether we have a problem that is peculiar to Britain. Our culture is indeed very resistant. Some believe that this had something to do with the fact that we are subjects, not citizens, but Jeff Kipnis negated this theory by his comments on the Trooping of the Colour Ceremony, which he attends annually in order to give inspiration to his teaching work at the Architectural Association.

Some of us thought that the problem was rather that the British tend to be back-room-boffins inventing radar, and that we are essentially small-time nuts, happier in the back yard than in the public library.

Peter Cook advanced the point of view that the English are an island race, a race of eccentrics and in that sense essentially private individuals. Well, I am not sure that this argument would go very far, because there have been British artists who have made art that is unchangeable in the home – for example, Francis Bacon, who terrifies me far more than Picasso ever did. Maybe it turns out that our cultural resistance to art is more to do with the fact that we do not mind art, but when it comes to architecture, we question if it can really be considered art. It is paid for by the client, and can the client truly pay for a person just to express him or herself? It evidently happens in America, so I think that is the root question for us Brits. Are we really willing to accept architecture as an art?

I have to say that the Royal Academy – this is a small fleeting punch for the RA – has done well because the Summer Show now includes architecture in a way it has never done before. I think we must give a lot of credit to Hugh Casson and Philip Dowson for carrying on the good work. An exhibition of British architecture over the last three Summer Shows is about to travel the States, so we will find out if they think we are unduly inhibited in a cultural sense.

Nevertheless, I think it is difficult for us to accept that architecture is an uninhibited art and that art is full of crazy form. We owe a special debt to Frank for showing us crazy art. I went to Paris recently to look at the nearest Gehry building to Camden Town, and I was pleasantly surprised. The American Center on first sight was wild, but once the eye becomes used to it, it really is very beautiful. It conforms to the backness of the back, to the Frenchness of the Boulevard, and round the side it gradually grows more American until there is a kind of 'Welcome Bill Clinton' note on the garden side. It should be said that in its earlier form it had one of those moving images, just like the Terragnis scheme for the Dantem, or like Richard Rogers' original scheme for the Pompidou Centre. Frank chose to clad his building not in crocodile hide but in stone, and stone has a way of bringing everything into culture.

So in conclusion I would say the debate was about training, about how the artist was brought into culture. Should the artist put out a completely alien message that stands for a transformed society with transformational architecture that does not compromise; or should the architect mediate within himself between the new and the old, and try to show at least one path by which the new can be mediated and brought into the old.

I think this is the way Frank has chosen to follow – he won the debate today because at the end there was general recognition of the limitations of architecture, especially when just one building is added to a city. I think we follow Frank's wisdom when we agree with him that the architect with his one building can change the scene, but he cannot with that one building transform society. Frank you have changed the scene, we love your stuff, please come again.

Gehry's Relevance For Britain

A Debate

Jeff Kipnis, Charles Jencks, Robert Maxwell and Maggie Toy

BRITISH REPRESSION, AMERICAN OPENNESS?
Charles Jencks

Frank Gehry activates the repressive reflex in certain British critics who have tied their flag to High-Tech. Martin Pawley condemns the Vitra Centre Villa as 'a monster cottage' and 'mad munchkin' architecture, and for looking too cheap and being too expensive. Deyan Sudjic attacks the Minneapolis Museum as 'extreme expressionism' and 'the architecture of egotism'. Perhaps no-nonsense utilitarianism has replaced puritanism and eighteenth-century good taste, as the stick to whip creative architects into line.

Robert Maxwell

In Britain, on the one hand, there is the extreme of modernism in High-Tech, while on the other hand, there is a reactionary movement being led by high-profile figures such as Quinlan Terry and the Prince of Wales. Both sides argue about technology and cost; the former is eager to make the most of state-of-the-art methods which include the use of lasers in architecture, which involves a certain risk but it is invigorating; whilst the latter argues that risk does not apply to a social art like architecture. Hence, only tried and tested technology, which has been proven to work over time, should continue to be used, modified only slightly if necessary. So both arguments stem from technology and cost. Yet, in an international context there is a big difference in comparison to America: the English situation shows more signs of repression.

Jeff Kipnis

Up to the point that you say that there is a cultural difference expressed in the architecture, I am in agreement, and I think this difference deserves attention. But, when you argue that the nature of the difference is that the English are repressed, I become uncomfortable.

Of course, one recognises the virtue of the argument; yet I cannot subscribe to the notion that the British are labouring under the weight of a repression that prohibits them from achieving what they really want to achieve, while the Americans are more inclined to do what they really want. I do not think that portrays a fair picture of either the British or the Americans, nor a sufficient understanding of the nature of repression.

Robert Maxwell

Irrespective of any more cut throat differences between the British and the Americans, there is another more general sense in which culture oppresses: we receive certain unspoken commandments and it requires a real effort to break them. I am talking about the rule of the word, the logos. This works through natural language. Britons and Americans are equally repressed by English, but with certain differences. Maybe the Burmese consider the British, French and Americans to be equally peculiar. In other words there is no one absolutely neutral human cultural viewpoint.

Jeff Kipnis

Once you start the question of cultural relevance two elements surface, cultural context and structure. It is not clear whether the structure of a given context is equivalent to the repression of that context. I think that we should not blindly start with the assumption that cultural structure is tantamount to repression.

Charles Jencks

In British architecture there is a form of self-censorship: architects attempt to fit in with the cultural norms of utilitarianism, reticence, understatement and privatism. These are the meta-codes which emerged in the eighteenth century throughout British society and I do think they are evident in High-Tech. After all, what is

High-Tech, if not, on a certain level, a capitulation to the idea of technological authentication. Technology validates architecture in the same way as in America, exhibiting in the Museum of Modern Art validates you as an architect. What validates people in this country is an appeal to 'long life with low cost'. Or low energy or a host of things which focus around Jeremy Bentham's utilitarianism. One has to turn to the seventeenth century to find architects such as Vanbrugh, Hawksmoor and Wren who spoke more directly of architectural values.

Utilitarianism seems to have dominated the Modern Movement since 1945, when the Labour Party announced the need to build a million houses, come what may; whether they were architectural or not was ruled unimportant. Architecture was hence considered, like the health service, a social service, and that established the popular discourse about serving people, of which Norman Foster is a strong advocate. His utilitarianism is, I believe, ultimately spiritual – or what I have called 'transcendental materialism', because it is so reverential about handling materials in a sacred, austere light – but you will not find anyone discussing these spiritual aspects because of the same British repressions.

Maggie Toy

The particular national influences and histories might be different; you are outlining a history in Britain which has led to this, but it happens all over the world.

Robert Maxwell

Charles has a point. I went to University College, London for twenty years where they placed Jeremy Bentham on display once a year. He is very much a local saint and wheeling his effigy out annually is a local tradition.

From those years I remember Claude Lévi-Strauss giving a couple of talks in front of British anthropologists and being heckled to the point where he almost had to stop talking. Why? Because he was erecting theories and generalising without sufficient authority. He was suggesting an interesting idea but could not prove it, which the anthropologists immediately leapt upon. So there is a British tradition which distrusts theory and wants everything to be difficult, a tradition that relates to the utilitarian only when absolutely necessary.

Jeff Kipnis

High-Tech is about image, pure and simple. On the other hand, let us not underestimate the value of image.

Charles Jencks

Nevertheless, the High-Tech architects really think they are performing a social service. It is ideologically important for them to believe that their work represents the cheapest, most functional and most technological service. Sometimes it is the cheapest! The first building that Foster designed for computer technology in 1970 went up in three minutes and you cannot be cheaper than that. With the Hong Kong Bank he produced the most expensive building in the world. Of course, at times Frank Gehry also justifies his buildings as 'cheapskate' and admits that others, for instance, for Peter Lewis, are too expensive. We live in a world where cost is politicised and is itself used to repress architecture. After all, the Pantheon, the Parthenon and Chartres each cost the equivalent of £30 billion. We live not in a nation of shopkeepers, but cultural-money-squeezers.

Jeff Kipnis

Every project built comes in on a budget.

Charles Jencks

Who says?

Jeff Kipnis

Eisenman, for example. What he does not say is that he spends two-thirds of his time doubling and tripling the budget.

Robert Maxwell

That is PR.

Jeff Kipnis

I think these arguments are legitimate. I just wonder if utilitarianism and its repercussions are the questions we want to work out.

Charles Jencks

No, it is just one of the questions which Frank Gehry's presence forces upon the British. He raises the question of functionalism in a new way which is not stereotyped. His buildings, especially the offices, are very cheap and functional in a way that High-Tech is not.

Robert Maxwell

I think we need to discuss Charles' point about British repression further because it is relevant to polemics in this country. You have to recognise what is so special about it and if it is even partly true – which makes it worth commenting on. Words have the tremendous ability to oppress, so when there is general oppression in the world we understand that it is largely engineered by the spoken and written word.

Jeff Kipnis

Repression, as I understand it, occurs when a desired activity is not pursued out of fear of punishment, whether legal, social or psychological. The mere absence of an activity in and of itself is not *prima facie* evidence of repression. The marked preference for saris and the absence of polyester pant suits among women in India does not indicate that Indian women are repressed; more likely, it is indicative of the cultural forces of tradition. Only if Indian women really wanted to wear polyester pant suits but were prohibited from doing so by law, fear of censure or humiliation could one meaningfully speak of repression.

Likewise, the mere absence among English contemporary architects of tendencies that might be likened to Gehry would only be indicative of repression if some of these architects were prohibited from pursuing such an architecture against their will. It probably makes sense to speak of the Victorian English as sexually repressed by a pervasive moral code, since one imagines that they really wanted to pursue sex more than they were allowed. But to say that contemporary English architects are repressed because they are limited in moral code does not seem an apt comparison to me. Is the relative absence of High-Tech among American architects indicative of a repression or of a lack of moral commitment to function? Neither, I believe.

NEO-EXPRESSIONISM?
Robert Maxwell

Jeff, there is another level in between, in which we have to say that the whole of the Modern Movement was itself a Puritan revolution within the idea of socialism and social betterment. Especially during – and even after – the Heroic Period of the 1920s, the theory was always a functionalist one. Those who pushed it too far and came up with Expressionist architecture, such as Hugo Häring, Eric Mendlesohn and Hans Scharoun were always a minority. Their work incorporated too much expression. In a certain way Expressionism became an undercurrent throughout the Modern Movement. We have books on

Expressionism because it can be dealt with as a limited field within the general field of Modern architecture. What we are finally seeing with Frank is some kind of freeing of the Expressionist libido that was theoretically freed in the Modern Movement, but was in practice repressed by our theory of functionalism. Hence I see a puritan European development separate from the British.

Jeff Kipnis

Up to a point I agree. You are correct to infer that the rationalist strain of Modernism established a prevailing context in which a certain set of idiosyncratic work was marginalised under an uncritical rubric, Expressionsim. But I have serious doubts about the historical treatment of the so-called Expressionists, in particular about those arguments that see the architecture as pursuing a freedom of expression. I believe Scharoun's work, for example, was more concerned with existential politics than some lyrical notion of expression.

I make this point because I do not believe that Gehry's work, or for that matter many of the others that are treated by critics today as neo-Expressionist, is adequately approached with the meagre critical tools of the historical concept of Expressionism.

I would like to recall Robert Evans' comparison of Gaudi and Mies. Robert's argument was essentially that the Barcelona Pavilion is not truly rational, but was, in fact, an image of structural rationality, over-structured in some places and under-structured in others. Gaudi's work, on the other hand, often cited as a key example of Expressionism in architecture, and therefore irrational in some sense, was in every way, save its appearance, rational. Modernism grasped and laid claim to the image of rationality, and then enhanced that image with claims to a social project, the project of betterment. But the capacity of Modernism to claim both the name of rationality and social engagement, and therefore to marginalise a series of deviant architectures as Expressionist, means that we have to pay attention to those deviant tendencies today, to re-emergence in terms that are different from those established by Modern criticism.

Let me add that both Charles' and Bob's assumption is that any structure, by virtue of its processes, in retrospect always seems to be repressive. Charles and Bob play with the language of repression, a play made possible by, and limited by language structures. We always have to be attentive to the cost of those limitations without

disregarding the value of structure. Those instances which emerge and antagonise a prevailing structure – such as something called Expressionism – are always categorised as deviant. They are therefore initially more important for their categorical deviations than for their specific individual attributes. Consider the group we were asked to compare: Alsop, Gough and Gehry. The assumption was that these architects are alike in their inclination to deviate, rather than the more important architectural question of what each of them offers.

Charles Jencks

The discussion between Alsop, Gough and Gehry brings me back to the model of three different kinds of relationships between individual talent and tradition. Theoretically we all want a situation in which we have a high degree of cultural coherence *and* a developed culture in which a lot is expressed. Because of a developed culture, people have conventional manners, they speak of love and the desires of the universe: they need many languages to do that. That ideal culture is a *positive-sum-game*. You can use a language creatively and you are not held back, but liberated by it. Now the usual thing is the *zero-sum-game* where you get a kind of trade-off – say, in London recently, 'if we are going to have an expressive piece of Richard Rogers in the *Channel 4* building, then we have to counter it by a second-rate urbanism all around it'. The British context is loaded with such trade-offs and it will allow only a token Expressionism. However, the *minus-sum-game* is sadly the most prevalent with, characteristically, a competition between the traditionalism of Prince Charles, the avant-gardism of Zaha Hadid, and the populism of the developers. The legal situation demands some compromise, which is half Hadid, half Prince Charles and half vernacular. Three-halves are a *minus-sum-game*; all three are unhappy. In a confused culture, that game is the greatest danger. Gehry's work shows you can have a *positive sum-game* if you good architects are picked out, given good commissions, *and* are then, yourselves, attentive to the context – the American Center is probably an example of that.

THE AMERICAN CENTER AND VITRA MUSEUM
Charles Jencks

Critics have complained that the American Center is not bold and Californian enough, that Gehry has 'abandoned

PAGE 54: The binoculars at Chiat Day, Venice, California, 1975/1986-91; FROM ABOVE: The American Center, Paris, 1988/91-93; Vitra Factory and Museum, Weil am Rhein, Germany, 1987/88-89

his wild spontaneous quality in order to cater to a Parisian norm'. The result is 'more ordinary and less powerful than his other buildings', as *Time* magazine has put it.

Robert Maxwell

There is a sense in which at the American Center Gehry was 'good' on the side of the Boulevard and so could afford to be 'naughty' on the side facing the park. Hence the building is, in a sense, compromised (maybe in the way Will Alsop used the word) in order to hook it into the present day norm. As a pragmatic step to make it acceptable, Gehry plays it down on one side and then plays it up on the other, just like Piers Gough. That is my view of how an individual act of building can attempt to recognise limitations and still express freedom all in one act and on one site. But you seem to want the new building or group of buildings to be uncompromising, in the sense that they must succeed in demonstrating something different from hanging on to the existing norm, and indeed be seen to be rejecting it completely.

Jeff Kipnis

I do not think Gehry's work really has anything in particular to do with his being from California in a rationalist sense. Rather, it solicits, out of that context, latent possibilities which were not previously evident, activating them in such a way as to show that there was, in fact, already another rational context. If you look at Gehry's own house, the Wagner House, Chiat Day, or especially the Disney Concert Hall – all of them have done something quite spectacular. They produce what first appears to be a sculptural object, but upon further inspection you discover that they redefine the context by finding relationships that were latent, but not active in one's current understanding of it. In Paris, on the other hand, I think Bob's account is absolutely accurate. Gehry apologetically re-enforced our understanding of the prevailing context, merely adding gesture.

Robert Maxwell

If I could just comment on Vitra. It is the one building which I wrote about in my book without actually visiting. But I reconstructed just how the complex corners of the shed could combine with the complexity of the entrance group to suggest a longer entity. Gehry himself refers to the idea of a campus which would be formally coherent by comparison with the back of the

shed. Grimshaw's building is quite different, as it is exactly the dead-pan shed that the client wanted; whereas with Gehry's Vitra building one is under the impression that the shed is a reflection of Gehry's *own* composition. The way the volumes work in the interior of the Vitra building suggests that there is a certain organisation of forms, particularly in the cruciform top lighting, which seems to be a re-working of something naggingly familiar.

Jeff Kipnis

I agree. Gehry changed the whole language of the context.

Robert Maxwell

It is different from the work outside the scheme; the building is constructed within his own language, within which he is referring to his own points of reference.

Charles Jencks

I would like to pose the opposite case. I think all Gehry's buildings show this double structuring, they all have a tendency to have a side which is over-designed and expressive, and a side which is understated and vernacular. They all have fronts and backs, so the Paris building is not so much unique, as canonic. I believe the French critics and others are objecting to the reference; Gehry discusses two aspects in particular: first, the context of Parisian housing which no longer exists – the masonry context of punched-hole windows to which the back of his building relates. Secondly, Gehry discusses the opposition between cleavage in the slate roofs of the Hôtel de Ville and the slate and limestone combination of the building in Paris. He takes the very code which the French *avant-garde* despises, because it has been done to death. If he built in London in an analogous manner we could chastise his fitting into London Georgian; but Gehry is a Californian who lived in Paris for several years and fell in love with precisely those things that bore some Parisians. These people find the code he is quoting too bourgeois, well known, and omnipresent. That is the main difference between the American Center and his Californian buildings, and I think the great thing about Frank is that he can rise above associations and say, 'I don't care too much what the code is, I want to make comments on it'. In that sense, I agree with Jeff, he finds out what is available and what is not so obvious.

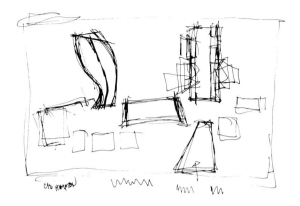

Robert Maxwell

I rather agree with that. Frank is of a Jewish background and at a certain moment he both rebelled against it and was forced to rediscover it: that is his own account, and there is a sense in which he is very earthy. He is not a cerebral *avant-garde* architect. He may, in Charles' terms be the first 'Deconstructionist', but I doubt whether he falls into the Deconstructionist band in terms of defining an architecture to criticise the status quo. He is not particularly interested in doing so.

CHIAT DAY
Charles Jencks

I would like to discuss the built sketches for Chiat Day. Frank manages to continue the frenzy, passion and sexuality of his initial sketches into his built work, a terrifically important part of what he is communicating. I do not know why other architects cannot do the same. They all sketch, but Frank seems to be the only one (besides Koolhaas and Starck) who manages to carry the energy through to the finished product.

  Frank is at his best, as in the Chiat Day conversion of a warehouse, when he is playing dialectically against something else. The spatial layering and the use of contrast in this conversion is very important as well – especially the shiny set against very dull materials. Frank enjoys playing with our senses, teasing them into wondering where reality stops and starts; in Chiat Day he has created a wonderful village which houses an extraordinary amount of art collected by the client. But one never knows where Frank is stopping and an artist is starting. He blurs categories, crosses boundaries and thus the building becomes the most heteromorphic and 'dialogical' I can think of. You cannot tell what is what, as in any convivial city which mixes function and types. The most contemplative space is a small room which is patterned with corrugated furniture. It is a sacred space so quiet you can hear your heart beat.

SCHNABEL HOUSE
Robert Maxwell

What about the $3 million Schnabel House?

Charles Jencks

Every actor who is famous in Los Angeles has to build a shrine, a museum to keep their memorabilia. The Schnabel House is another outstanding example of inspired contrast and, furthermore, Frank has here managed to invent the most scaleless and awkward window ever designed. This forces you to revalue notions of beauty and what a very simple, over-scaled window can be, and how it can transform into poetry the brutality of a one-room box.

Jeff Kipnis

I think Frank's recent buildings begin to show a strategy in which large incongruent gestures are brought into a more coherent relationship through rigorous, but non-platonic geometry, organisation and material detail. Gehry's Vitra masterplan, museum and factory produce a new organisational space – a space I find interesting. It engages a prevailing organisational and formal geometry with an object that is both incongruent to the prevailing incoherent formal language and incoherent with the prevailing organisation, and then maps out very slow mechanisms by which the museum re-establishes a new coherence without losing its formal incongruity.

Gehry's factory was a reiteration of Grimshaw: it had to be identical, it had to sit exactly in the rigid geometry and match the material. He then introduced the two staircases which start to modify the entire organisational structure of the site. This new, more complex geometry incorporates Grimshaw's old language and the museum into a new mode of coherence.

Robert Maxwell

I see the staircases as supporting actors which create a campus and therefore give a field of depth. It seems to me Jeff, that when you compare the deadpan factory with the sculptural elements in front of it, you are enjoying what you see as a contrast and which I see as an incongruity. This incongruity is neither here nor there, from Frank's point of view. The fact is that Frank enjoys creating certain kinds of sculptural forms and he has done something which is sympathetic to his own ideas, which have certain ramifications. First of all he designed a very sculptural building, with parts of it leaning out and about. He is putting a kind of dance into movement, all the way from the inclined show cases and shelves to the architecture, which is like another universe. The point I want to stress is not the incongruity of this but the coherency of it – there is a certain passage (I have forgotten where it is from) where Frank describes his building as a system of relationships, as if it were a language system. The coherency is enormous and once you lose your normal references and work into

it, you enjoy it. It is only then that you wonder what the principles are that give it such coherence. Sculptural dance is only possible if the building is not a block, it has to be broken down into entities, like this factory or a monastery. As with the latter, at Vitra he encloses a central space with a tilted crucifix form which reminds us of Byzantine architecture.

Hence, I would claim that there are certain regularities in culture which are transformed and displaced into new situations in order to allow a new coherency to develop.

Robert Maxwell

You cannot invent a *completely* new coherence, but only be modifying one that we already recognise. It is creative and different, not the usual run-of-the-mill stuff.

Jeff Kipnis

In the museum, Gehry uses a formal element which appears as a secondary feature to the primary language of factory complex. All the factories have mechanical boxes and secondary elements, which he turns into primary features of the museum. He nearly reiterates a cloister geometry and a central axis, but more importantly, he loosens it so as to not repeat the type, a tactic typical to accreted urban and campus organisations in the US.

Robert Maxwell

Now here is an interesting point. You are claiming that the USA has a peculiar condition.

Jeff Kipnis

I think America has a different structure to that in Europe, but that does not mean it is progressive.

Robert Maxwell

All right, it is different.

Jeff Kipnis

I do not think that the Macy's Thanksgiving Day Parade is any less repressive than the Trooping of the Colour. They are two completely different organisational strategies.

Robert Maxwell

No, what I am saying is that if you look at the points on the inner side of the museum from a point on the road, you think you are seeing something different from what

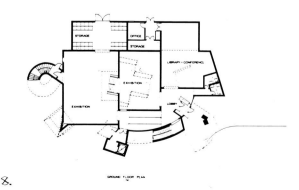

8.

ABOVE and CENTRE: The Schnabel House, Brentwood, California, 1986-89;
BELOW: Vitra Factory/Museum, Weil am Rhein, Germany, 1987/88-89

is really there: it is an illusion where you think you are seeing a total reversal of movement and sculpture.

Charles Jencks

The Vitra Museum is the first example of Frank's vermiform coming out and being very consciously expressed. We are close to Ronchamp, to Dornach of Rudolf Steiner and the Expressionist tradition in Europe, figuratively and in terms of place. Just as Frank is aware of European history and relating to the Parisian context, you have to see this as a petite Ronchamp for furniture, and therefore implicitly as a place for the worship of furniture. Does the sacred role legitimise it for the client?

Secondly, you have to see it as a Southern Baroque church which uses reflected light and light scoops – which of course Ronchamp does too. But the wonder of Southern Baroque is that you often cannot tell where the light is coming from because it is so diffused. The whiteness is important here as it allows Frank to create a fluid surface, which is underscored by the vermiform which unifies everything.

This unity should be contrasted with the Winton Guest House, an extreme example of the opposite case, where Frank used five different shape-grammars. He played a compositional game which was close to the painter Morandi, saying, 'let's take these five different objects and push them together into this one still life'. And then, suddenly, 'no, let's go all white and start to contort my objects so they're twisted'. It is as if the objects have been squeezed and fused together, in both colour and volume. Hence I see the acknowledgement of history here and both Baroque and Expressionist religious codes, all pulled towards fluid unity.

Jeff Kipnis

Einstein was very close to Newton but they were different and that is the whole point: it is the difference that is important. Gehry is very close to the history of Western architecture and works with it and against it, but the difference is more important than the similarity.

Robert Maxwell

But the similarities and the differences go together: you could not see one without the other.

Jeff Kipnis

The similarities enable the differences, but it is the differences that have to command our critical attention.

Charles Jencks

Spoken like a true market-man: 'in the economic market it is the difference that makes the difference', nothing else sells.

Jeff Kipnis

Chiat Day is not 'new and improved Byzantine architecture', nor is the Winton House 'new and improved'. To my mind it is uninteresting Tuscan architecture. To take an initial condition such as any of the types which you cited – the organisational types, the institutional types or the formal types – and use it to understand Frank's project, I prefer to ask: what new thing does this do, that its typological precedent did not do? Your taxonomic inclination overwhelms your examination of the work. We need to elucidate the generative structure of each project, of Vitra and Chiat Day, and then compare them to the American Center. I think that unlike the first two, the latter actually completes the generative structure of its context rather then reopening it.

VERMIFORM UNITY vs HETERO-ARCHITECTURE
Charles Jencks

It is in the unifying projects of Frank – all the three you mention, plus Disney – that his shape-grammar develops. As an architect opens up a new language – always very exciting – he carries a whole set of people behind him who exploit the same language from different positions. We can argue about what exactly the shape-grammar is: I feel it has some possibilities and some problems that his previous grammar did not have. Let us call the new grammar 'crystalline worms'. Vitra was the first project in which Frank used crystalline worms and then at the American Center and Disney.

Jeff Kipnis

I think we should note that right after Vitra, Peter Eisenman designed the Columbus Convention Centre.

Charles Jencks

Yes, Peter's worm come after Frank's, but he caught worms from Hejduk rather than Frank.

Jeff Kipnis

But Peter makes them do something very different, so here we have a good example of learning what a new kind of architecture can achieve.

Charles Jencks

A very interesting dialectic ensued between Eisenman, Koolhaas and Hadid when they saw Gehry using his vermiforms. They were jealous because he was doing it, he was there first, he opened the way to what some people called the New Baroque. Of course that is a very reductive way of looking at it, but I want to turn to the consequences of this shift. What is lost in this is the heterogeneity of the Winton Guest House and Chiat Day. For me the Disney Hall and the American Center are slightly less interesting than they would have been had the grammar been slightly more disjunctive – which some of Frank's models show. On the other hand, I find it interesting that the final shape-grammar is much more like landscape or, to be precise, landscape of planes under extreme tension. This is an architecture of colliding, tectonic plates, squeezing against each other before warping, prior to an earthquake. It is also an architecture which is fairly easy to build because these are only slightly warped, dumb boxes.

Maggie Toy

What do you mean by 'dumb box'?

Charles Jencks

I mean a box with a 'stupid' window in it, you know one of his dimensionless windows, as at the Schnabel House. His volumes are often just boxes, very simple to build with stud walls; but they are 'dumb' because there is no further articulation, proportion or detail. There are four or six walls in a primitive structure and then Frank brings light into them in all sorts of unconventional and surprising ways. So the finished result is never a dumb box. But by starting with one, it means he can keep it under control with low costs.

Robert Maxwell

So what is the problem? You said you had a problem.

Charles Jencks

No, I said the problem was the loss of heterogeneity, with the unified style.

Robert Maxwell

You cannot imagine the whole universe made like this?

Charles Jencks

Not the universe so much as each of Frank's buildings,

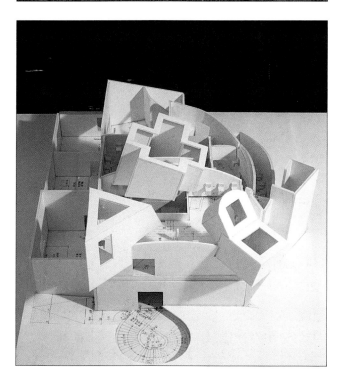

Vitra Factory and Museum, Weil am Rhein, Germany, 1987/88-89

which I have referred to. The Disney Hall should have had more than a two-material dialectic between glass and steel – Expressionist works and masonry – and the American Center, which is more or less the same thing, needs a third material or aesthetic. I am asking for a bit more heterogeneity here, which is evident in his models and earlier intentions.

Jeff Kipnis

Just two minutes ago you agreed that the vermiform geometry had a generating capacity which caused new organisational effects. I think we also tacitly agreed that it is not Expressionist. Therefore you have to stop calling them Expressionist. It is not about expressing and it is certainly not about expressing individuality.

Charles Jencks

Bob asked why I have a problem with this, and my answer is that it changes an emphasis in this direction. Frank opened the whole discourse on extreme heterogeneity in a very exciting way. For example, the early work in the 80s, such as the Loyola Law School or Chiat Day, with its binoculars, has six different forms in juxtaposition.

Robert Maxwell

I would not have thought Chiat Day was an example of heterogeneity – it seems to me to be sculpturally unified.

Charles Jencks

The building has binoculars, ship buildings and trees as generative images and a further congruence of industrial, vernacular and funk elements. So, the later, more unified grammar is problematic because it tends toward the aesthetic (and I hope you understand I am using this as a classification). There is an aestheticism which smoothes over some distinctions and differences in a way which is like other contemporary architecture. Of course I too like aesthetic unity and am not arguing for over-fragmentation. But I am arguing for the incorporation of difference and different urban experience. The danger of the Disney Hall, the American Center, and the late vermiform work is that it is extremely interesting as generative grammar, but oversimplifying and aesthetising.

Robert Maxwell

Why is that a danger?

Charles Jencks

With someone like IM Pei, Kenzo Tange or Richard Meier, we get a whole environment in a unified aesthetic.

Robert Maxwell

Do we mind what happened to Richard Meier?

Charles Jencks

As a programme for a large environment like the Getty Center it can be questioned.

Jeff Kipnis

I think what Charles is saying is that Richard Meier uses a very limited repetoire of spatial types. The difference between the two is simply the difference between a rich organisation of space and a very destitute organisation.

Robert Maxwell

I object to Charles' use of the word 'danger' because it implies we are being led in a wrong direction, that we should regret it; whereas I thought that Charles' whole view was a pluralist one. Like India absorbing the West, everything should be absorbed and go into nothingness, except for those things which are seeding and are going to have a renaissance. Hence, we do not have to worry about the bad, as it will be disciplined.

Charles Jencks

For me pluralism is critical, and there is always an agenda; it is not a case of 'anything goes'.

Robert Maxwell

I have the same difficulty with 'critical pluralism' as with 'critical regionalism'.

Maggie Toy

We obviously all agree that Frank introduced something new with the Vitra Museum and that other people are adopting his grammar. Yet you are saying that was the point in time when he started going wrong.

Charles Jencks

No, the difference is between going wrong and a 'danger'. I am merely saying that there is a danger of aestheticism, not that Frank has fallen into it. Let me put it this way: what is wrong with the American Center? The fact is that there are no words, advertisements or images on the billboard which hangs over the front, which Frank designed as an integral part of his language of difference. The Center becomes merely aesthetic, it does not have the other languages which it so sorely needs: the language of commerce, of the missing restaurant, of the missing neon and of *The American in Paris*; all the languages which would activate it. The Center is slightly too unified, like a sculptural statement, because it was not completed to Frank's design.

Robert Maxwell

You see that as a danger, yet with the Vitra Museum, I see it as a typical Modern statement. By that I do not mean that Modernism conforms to an exact style, but to an exact attitude which is basically one that would recognise crucial steps on a downward or upward path. This depends on how you look at it: there are many scales, from institutional mediation and liberation through religion, to individual liberation through experience. Why do Americans dress informally compared to Europeans? Throughout history there is a sense of progression starting with Augustus occupying the temple and making it into a palace. The tradition is a kind of cultural thermodynamics, of entropy, and in this sense I believe very strongly that museums and places of display have taken over a lot of the functions that were formally provided by religious institutions. An aesthetic experience is offered now as an element of spiritualisation; this is what it is about in dramatic and total terms.

Jeff Kipnis

What Charles has identified as 'dangerous', I believe to be 'a most important and promising future'.

Robert Maxwell

Well, you have something in common that I do not have, because I do not see the danger.

Maggie Toy

That makes it dangerous.

Charles Jencks

That is a really interesting point – we have identified a key juncture in the discussion. I accept that the Vitra Museum is a significant opening up of those ideas of space, light and so forth, but that is why I said that it is 'aesthetic'. This is only a 'danger', not a 'failure'. I think

American Center, Paris, France, 1991 - 93

American Center, Paris, France, 1991-93

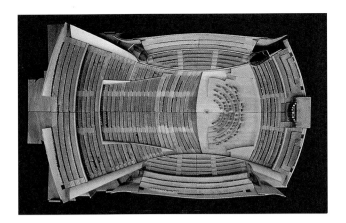

Model of the Disney Hall, Los Angeles, 1988/92-97

the Vitra Museum is a wonderful building and I agree with your remarks, Jeff, about its generative capacities. It is interesting that Bob and I agree on the spiritual subtext and Jeff, you appear not to mind when Vincent Scully brings up a spiritual reading.

Robert Maxwell

Common and ordinary people are very important when it comes to creating and making an atmosphere.

Charles Jencks

What about their reaction to the spirituality of the interior?

Robert Maxwell

In Japan it is Buddhist light, in Europe it is Byzantine light – whatever you like.

Charles Jencks

Well, the metaphysics of light as Louis Kahn always used to say, carries different kinds of spiritual messages of hope, energy . . .

Robert Maxwell

All we have is life and death, light and dark, so light is extremely important.

Charles Jencks

The interiors remind me of the 1960s, La Dolce Vita and the architecture, of Supersensualism. These furniture objects in Vitra are displayed either in a row, as specimens, or as individual icons celebrating the ideal of furniture. Their logical structure is made manifest. Furniture itself is like a Euclidean proposition which you happen to sit on. That is why it is the ultimate fetish and the Vitra Museum really displays this spirituality of furniture, with each item completely decontextualised, as if in furniture heaven. The icons are not for sitting on – they are supposed to be understood as logical propositions and admired, not to be sat upon – that is why they are on plinths.

Robert Maxwell

There is something interesting in that because as the shelves go up they become less horizontal and more tipped and are therefore more theatrically presented. They reconceptualise the action of sitting. There are at least five ways in which the chairs are displayed: on shelves in frames, on podiums and then hung in different ways, and a variety of those ways is also related to the form of each chair. Again it is a disposition away from the trajectory which would like to put everything in its setting. They are abstracted.

Charles Jencks

Look at all the other furniture museums – particularly Richard Meier's in Frankfurt, or visit Habitat or Conran, and you will see the point. These chairs are all decontextualised, treated like abstract propositions of space, form and logic, and placed in frames up in the air as if they are religious paintings.

Robert Maxwell

You used the word 'decontexualisation', Jeff nodded and I agree. But what I see in that is a play of a universal appreciation that our civilisation has privileged abstract forms beginning with Cubism – although you can find abstraction earlier. We have a certain ability to abstract. Abstraction overlaps with representation and context, but the degree is always variable and I think what we have now is a degree of abstraction which we find congenial. We ought to talk about the Disney Building which seems much worse to me – more like a cartoon in a newspaper.

DISNEY HALL/ABSTRACT METAPHOR/KITSCH
Charles Jencks

The Disney Hall, which is half built, is on a very important site called Bunker Hill, which in the nineteenth century was an important, central site with some great houses. But Modernist renewal destroyed everything, the whole context of the nineteenth-century city was eaten up by one cultural monster after another. A new music centre of about 1968, in the American shopping centre style was designed, with a similar shopping monument on the other side, and Isozaki's Museum of Contemporary Art next to both. So you have four prestige buildings in an 'Art Acropolis'. This Modernist-Classical temple zone is surrounded by Downtown on one side, with very high rise buildings, and on the other by Chinese and Hispanic communities, and gang warfare. On the third side, the biggest amount of prisoners in the world – 45,000 criminals – are kept in a nearby prison. Hence, there is a tremendous heterogeneous mix of buildings and populations, with a consequent problem of maintaining high security.

Mike Davis' book, *City of Quartz*, among other things, had an effect just before this project was re-designed. Frank Gehry was tarred with the feather of designing buildings with chain-link which kept people out on the streets. So there was an obvious attempt here to open up the sides of the building with glass edges and invite people into a garden. But the garden has been cut down in the final scheme. Frank won the competition with one proposal, but because of the security problems and various other reasons, it has been simplified into this scheme. When it was sold to the people of LA, there was an outcry. About thirty per cent of those interviewed were put off, claiming it looks like squashed paper bags, things that had been thrown out in a Deconstructionist waste-paper basket, or 'LA after the Big One'. There is a great feeling among the red-necks and the hard hats – people who do not like this kind of thing – that this is a conspiracy of high culture.

Another set of metaphors came from the concerned ecologists, a strong vocal group who think the $150 million should have been spent on neighbourhood planning. Then there are Gehry's metaphors – the building as a ship and a Noah's Ark, because the interior is an ark for people to sit around and listen to music and the exterior has billowing sails. Also, like Scharoun's Philharmonic Hall in Berlin, he sees the interior as 'vineyards of people'. A metaphor which I, and the architectural critic Leon Whiteson have used, is the building as a galleon, sailing through LA. However, the people who disliked it compared it to the broken crockery of the painter, Julian Schnabel, and said, 'it's a con, like throwing broken crockery in the face of the public, an imposition of elitism'. There is, for Gehry, a series of other generative metaphors. If we look at the exterior it takes the vermiform and the box – the slightly inflated box – and turns these images into a growing flower, which naturally symbolises a growing, burgeoning culture.

Maggie Toy

But it is the same ilk as Vitra and the American Center.

Jeff Kipnis

Disney is the same ilk as Vitra, but it has nothing to do with the American Center – the only similarity it has with the latter is the use of unifying materials, but the Parisian geometries and quotations in the American Center are explicit. Vitra is my second favourite of his projects.

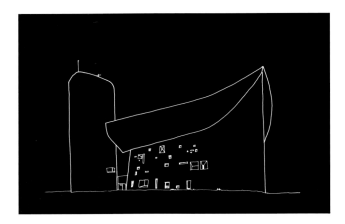

*Ronchamp. FROM ABOVE: Ronchamp, south elevation; Ronchamp Hands;
Ronchamp Duck*

What I am very interested in is not who can get the suggested imagery right – is it a flower, is it a sail, is it anything? Neither is it a choice in over-determination. It is not multiply-coded, it is not any of these things. It is the under-determined character of the geometry which gives it its capacity to engender a wide number of readings. It is actually quite a rigorous, though non-Euclidean geometry which enables a wide range of metaphors to be grafted onto it.

But to me the interesting thing is not the metaphor but the coherence of the geometry. Hence, it is a project about organisational space. There is a series of elements which we have become accustomed to in organising spaces: scales, large elements and small elements. It is very improbable that you can use those categories to understand this project – yet it is extremely coherent.

Robert Maxwell

I think that Frank could change a lot of those details.

Charles Jencks

Can I ask you what the difference is between under-determinism and Le Corbusier's Ronchamp?

Jeff Kipnis

Nothing. Ronchamp is underdetermined, not overdetermined, despite a history of criticism which holds the contrary.

Charles Jencks

I believe the multivalence of metaphors matters crucially, that all those metaphors I have mentioned are valid and they are all as interesting and relevant as they are at Ronchamp. One role of a mixed metaphor is to appeal coherently to different audiences with their different codes of perception. What is interesting about the Disney Hall is that it also transcends the metaphors I have mentioned, and that is important in the context of the political breakdown of LA. If the Disney Hall referred to any of the subcultures and classification systems explicitly, a specific group would read it as prejudicial. But it is powerful because it represents the growth of the unknown – something not yet codified. In that sense perhaps we agree by accident: what I call multivalence, Jeff calls under-determinism.

Robert Maxwell

I think it is kitsch.

Jeff Kipnis

You cannot set out to design under-determinism. You have to find an instrumental method. In fact the weakness of Frank's methods, the limitations of his methods, is that he begins with a figure and then systematically relaxes it.

Robert Maxwell

He does not do any mapping purely as a technique.

Charles Jencks

He models abstractions. He starts and comes back to a language which he is not intent on altogether creating. He does not mind if you see a galleon or an ark. The multivalence of the metaphors is, for me, over-unified at this scale in a single shape-grammar, but the Disney Hall is not kitsch because it is in an uncontaminated, unknown aesthetic.

Robert Maxwell

I think it is kitsch because it looks like a cartoon from the future. The forms of a building expanding to the top is a very common, low level paradigm for a perspective view. You see it constantly in cartoons: instead of buildings disappearing upwards, they expand upwards. It is reverse perspective, a common paradigm for expressing the future and that is why I consider it kitsch.

Charles Jencks

You mean a reference to a comic book makes it kitsch?

Robert Maxwell

He is referring to an absolutely low level common denominator, which is almost universal in America.

Charles Jencks

Is that good or bad?

Robert Maxwell

I did not say whether it is good or bad, I just think that is why it will be popular.

Charles Jencks

I accept that expansion upwards is a common sign of anti-gravitation, but the gesture is handled in a fresh way which avoids kitsch.

Maggie Toy

I do not think it is just a cartoon reference; is it not a reference about power?

Robert Maxwell

Absolutely. It is like one of those cartoon characters whose name I cannot remember, but the point I am trying to raise here is that Jeff's whole effort in the argument has been to suggest a certain kind of landscape, a certain position in culture, where you could begin to make a new context. He is resistant to our arguments. We are saying that Gehry's work is not completely new; you will always find that there is something old in there, something of Ronchamp. But his emphasis is on the newness and the possibilities that go on from that newness to make whole other new things.

Jeff Kipnis

For the last twenty years we have been concerned with incoherence and collapse as a positive project. Now we recognise a need for a coherence capable of organising diversity and congruency. I think that is where Frank has made a contribution. I do not think architecture's primary function is symbolic. I am particularly loathe to read the embedded cultural codes of a project. It is not that architecture is not open to that interpretation, it is just that those are the cultural effects that are not the architectural effects. Architecture has a very limited role, it has a contribution to make and I think Mike Davis really does not understand that.

Charles Jencks

When the LA populace accepts architecture of this importance into the centre of their public realm, they necessarily politicise it and lay a symbolic programme on it. You may not like it, but this building is now read as the symbol of a possibly unified culture, and the major architectural critic for the *LA Times*, Whiteson, interprets it as Gehry moving away from the Chiat Day heterogeneity towards unification. He also says this represents Gehry's maturity. Frank, are you more mature in this building than Chiat Day?

It is interesting that it has been interpreted in this way because in spite of Jeff's resistance to symbolism and reading architecture as a language, people are always going to do this. Architecture, as a public discourse, has to recognise this truth. But Jeff is also right – architecture

is much more than language and has obligations to generate purely architectural moves, so explicit and implicit metaphors are necessary.

Robert Maxwell

However, I would say that the binoculars at Chiat Day are an attempt by Frank to outmanoeuvre Oldenburg; they are a one-upmanship on Oldenburg – unless of course they represent Frank's own development as one of a group of artists. He is no longer concerned about showing himself to be level with them, he is concerned only with his own double entity.

Jeff Kipnis

The last point I would like to make is that I think we should not, as persons who are experts in the discipline, shy away from the importance of expertise. People react to Disney in the same way they first reacted to the Vietnam War Memorial. As we now know in the case of the latter, the experts were right and the public was wrong. Therefore, whether or not we collect the initial outcries/defences and try to arbitrate them, we also have to do something different, we have to exercise our best efforts as experts to guess the value of a project and judge the effects.

Robert Maxwell

I wanted to bring us back to the question of self-confidence and the lack of inhibition, because, Charles, you are very much identifying this as a response to an LA situation. Frank is being clever in the public realm to produce a symbol – or something seen as a symbol – but at the same time enjoying himself doing an even bigger building which is dancing around. On the one hand, it is self-confidence and on the other, it is awareness of a very wide audience in the US. It is a big country on the Pacific Rim. It has Latin America to bring into the trading, it has the frozen north which the Canadians guard, it has a much exposed position world-wide, and there is something in that more exposed position, I think, which, in a sense is Frank's birthright. He was born in Canada and came to LA – which makes him equal to a problem at a continental scale. In England, on the other hand, we have to say it is an island, offshore to Europe. It is not even sure if it is in Europe or part of the Atlantic Ocean, it is parochial by comparison and so the concerns of the ancient society that form it, always have to be justified in a utilitarian, or matter of fact way.

Chiat Day, Venice, California, 1975/86-91

In a way this is irrelevant to the question of architecture, but there are problems in England which one hopes will be resolved. But if this happens, it will not change the world. On the other hand, our speculations are more interesting at the level of world culture, which I believe we are approaching. I believe we are even approaching a situation where the problem for everyone will become the loss of belief, the loss of individuality, the loss of species, the loss of differentiation, and everything in a sense will become more and more superstructured. Like the Biosphere sort of extending out abstractly into outer space!

Charles Jencks

How do you see Disney Hall in that perspective?

Robert Maxwell

It is going to be very successful in LA terms.

Charles Jencks

It might have had a more liberating effect had it been built in London, because of what it would have meant to British architecture. It would have challenged the norm in a way Venturi's National Gallery failed to do, or for that matter, any building built in the last twenty years.

Robert Maxwell

Can you see the outcome of the South Bank competition resulting in a building like this?

Charles Jencks

Maybe in the case of Rogers' scheme, but only because the situation is already changing in the direction of Gehry, Alsop, Starck, Koolhaas *et al*. I think this is becoming more possible but we have not got there yet.

Jeff Kipnis

Some extraordinary buildings have been designed in England in their time, like the South Bank and the Royal College of Physicians. I do not think you can effectively analyse the problem with England by looking at something in the US.

Robert Maxwell

I must say I was touched by Charles' question because I can see the Disney Hall could never be built here, not in the next fifty years.

Charles Jencks

It is all about timing.

Robert Maxwell

It would be seen as vulgar in this country. But that points to a British problem: we are too small a country to be able to absorb big chunks of expression. That is why Europe is important, offering a kind of widening of our cultural horizons, introducing a scale that can answer back to America. In that sense we need more space to be truly transformational.

American Center

Paris, France

1991-1993

The fifty-six-year old American Center in Paris has earned itself a strong reputation in Europe as a centre of art and culture.

The recent addition to the Center is situated in the Bercy area, on a site bounded by the Rue Bercy, a new park and housing development and a landscaped plaza. In planning, the focus had to remain on the central purpose of the building – a meeting place for artistic and intellectual activities – whilst responding to the complex and diverse contextual conditions.

The lower levels of the buildings accommodate the most public functions of the Center, with multi-purpose performance spaces, shops, a restaurant, and a 400-seat theatre, all planned along the edge of the site to take advantage of accessibility from Rue Bercy and visibility to and from the park. Inside the building a great hall, the 'acceuil', unites all these functions, opening onto the park for special occasions.

Two discrete building forms in the upper levels house the more exclusive functions of the Center. To the west, penthouse duplexes crown an L-shaped apartment tower, with views of the Parisian skyline. To the east, an articulated block houses the fly-gallery to the theatre, a language school, administration offices, a library, and exhibition galleries which open out onto a rooftop sculpture terrace.

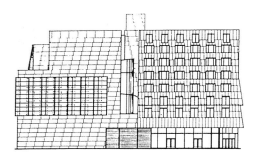

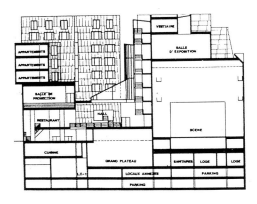

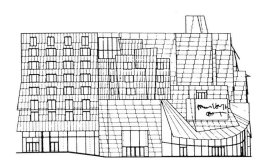

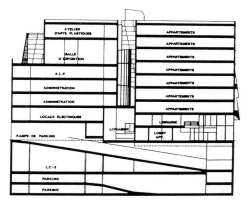

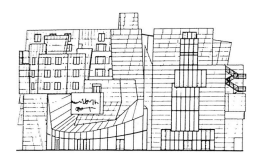

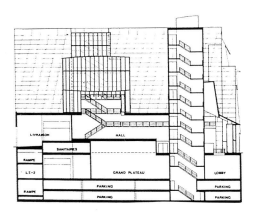

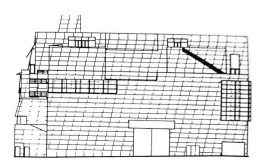

FROM ABOVE, L to R: North elevation; section; west elevation; section; south elevation; section; east elevation; section

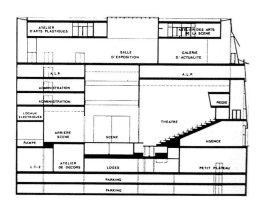

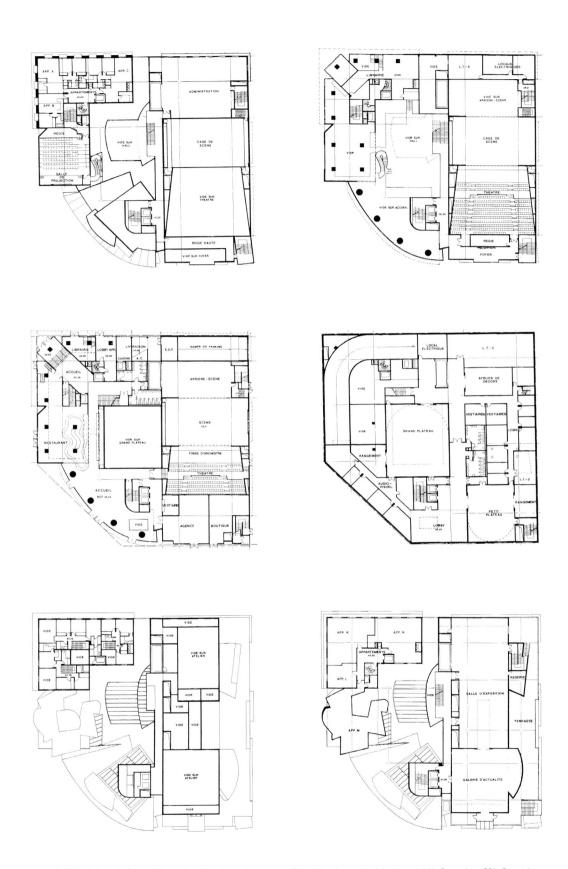

FROM ABOVE, L to R: Second floor plan; first floor plan; ground floor plan; lower level 1 plan; eighth floor plan; fifth floor plan

Concept sketch

New Headquarters for Vitra International, AG

Basle, Switzerland

1988/92 - 1994

The project is a master-planned development with the first phase being a 62,000 square foot new corporate office building. It is on a suburban site in Birsfelden, outside Basle, bounded by the low-rise Vitra manufacturing building on one side, and a small converted office structure on the other. The surrounding neighbourhood contains a mixture of light manufacturing, offices, houses and garden apartments. To the east is a dense forest reserve, visually tied to, but physically severed from, the site by an autobahn

submerged well below grade. The existing zoning required a building of less than ten metres in height. Parking was required at a rate of one car for every three employees on site, including existing uses.

Programmatically, the building is to house various working groups which require 'changeable' office planning in a way which will allow them to demonstrate and experiment with their own furniture lines. The offices also become showrooms, so a relatively neutral space was designed for this programme element. Much research

was done to investigate the state-of-the-art office space before the project began. As a result, 'combi office' and 'office landscape' types will be accommodated as well as more traditional closed and open offices. The strict energy codes of Switzerland do not allow air-conditioning in offices, so natural ventilation is accommodated by windows and the entirely shaded south wall under a large wing-shaped canopy.

In addition to the office block, there are more 'permanent' communal support areas such as the main entrance/reception, cafeteria, switchboard, mail, meeting and conference rooms. Since these spaces were thought of as less changeable and are used by all departments of the company, including off-site personnel, it was decided that they should be located centrally and allow for future expansion of offices around them. The nature of these spaces also allowed them to take on richer, sculpted shapes. The size and proportion of this element is similar to the scale of some of the existing homes nearby; it thus became dubbed 'the villa'. The wing canopy houses a 'living room' atrium and formally mediates between the simple office block and the central, energetic villa.

Architecturally, the building responds to the varied scale and conditions of its context. It welcomes visitors and workers alike and provides a strong, unique image for the company within its own work-space/showroom. The structure of the building is concrete and masonry. The external materials are a combination of painted stucco, zinc metal panels, and wood-framed doors and operable windows.

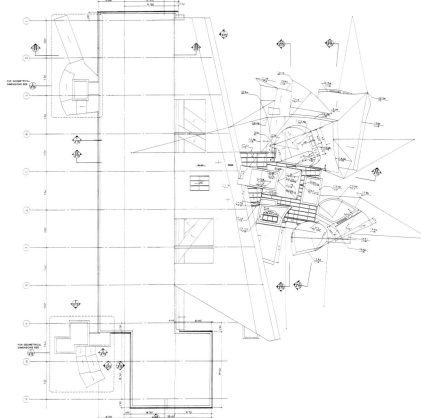

First floor plan

East elevation

South elevation

Walt Disney Concert Hall

Los Angeles, California

1988/92-97

Located on a historically and culturally prominent downtown site, the Walt Disney Concert Hall is to become the Los Angeles Philharmonic's permanent home. The Concert Hall will be situated on historic Bunker Hill at the intersection of First Street and Grand Avenue, adjacent to the existing Music Center of Los Angeles. The 200,000 square foot project began as an invitational design competition during which many of the fundamental design tenets were established. These included an open and accessible 'front door', a sympathetic and inclusive attitude in the building's relationship to the Music Center's existing Chandler Pavilion; a pedestrian scale frontage along Grand Avenue; a generous and open backstage/musician area and a large garden in which the Hall rests. Many elements have evolved since the competition, most notably the Hall's shape, the foyer size and the consideration and subsequent elimination of a chamber hall and a 350-room hotel.

The Concert Hall will now be located in the centre of the site, which consists of one city block. The majority of the site will be devoted to gardens, accessible not only from the Hall but from the adjacent streets, providing an oasis within the surrounding urban environment. An entry plaza will be located at the corner of First and Grand to relate the facility to the existing Music Center and a secondary entry plaza will be located at the corner of Second and Grand to provide primary access to the gardens. Unlike most concert halls, the building lobby will be dispersed along the street and will remain open during the day; large, operable glass panels will provide maximum accessibility to various amenities including a gift shop, a restaurant and café, access to the underground parking garage, and a pre-concert performance space. This area will be used for performance-related lectures, educational programmes and other scheduled and impromptu performances throughout the day.

The focus of the current design is the 2,4000-seat Concert Hall, whose interior and form are a direct expression of acoustical parameters, resulting in both visual and acoustic intimacy. Wood seating blocks surround the orchestra platform and, together with the sail-like wooden ceiling forms, give one the impression of a great ship within the plaster walls of the container. A pipe organ designed in conjunction with the interiors will occupy a central position between seating blocks at stage rear. Skylights and a large window in the rear of the Hall allow natural light to enhance daytime concerts.

The exterior of the Concert Hall will be clad in a flower-like wrapper of Italian limestone and stainless steel. The building's orientation, combined with the curving and folding exterior stone, will present highly sculptural compositions as viewers move along Grand Avenue and through the surrounding gardens and plazas. An extensive backstage technical area surrounds the Hall and opens onto a private musicians' garden. The backstage door will open onto a semi-public garden and the largest rehearsal room will be placed near this entry to be used for small-scale public performances. The openness of the backstage will encourage interaction between artists and the public. A 2,500-car garage on six levels will be constructed below the hall with access from three surrounding streets. Concert-goers will arrive in the foyer from the garage by way of an escalator cascade, which provides unique opportunities for art installations. Completion is scheduled for 1997.

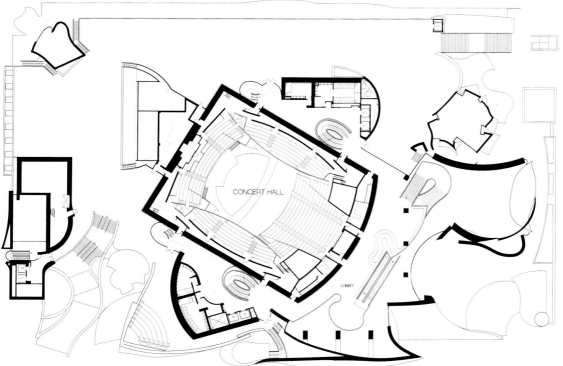

Garden level plan

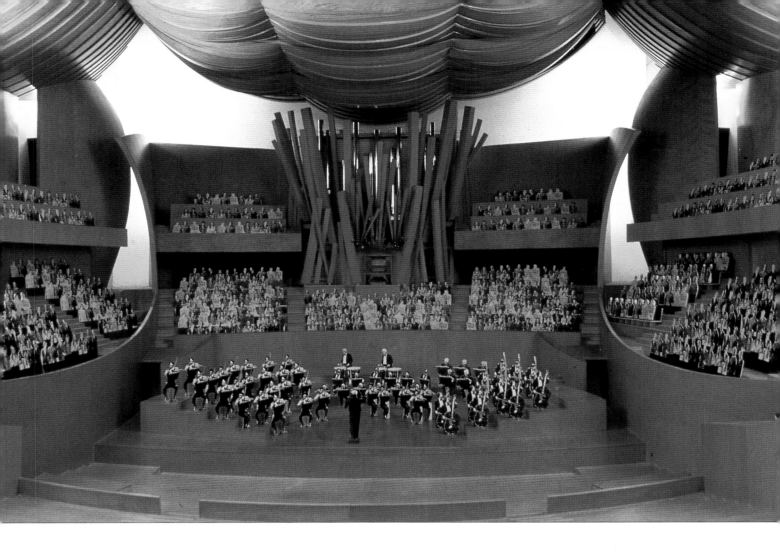

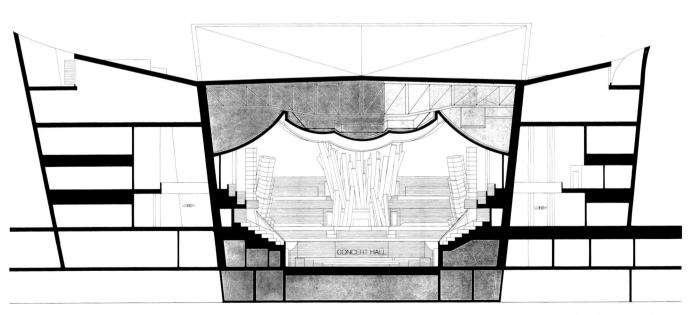

Transverse section of the concert hall

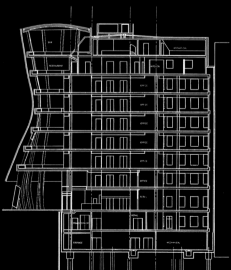

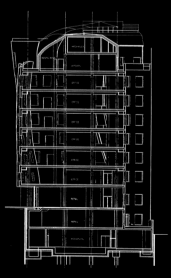

ABOVE, L to R: Eighth floor restaurant plan; ground floor site plan; BELOW, L to R: North elevation; west elevation

Nationale-Nederlanden Office Building

Prague, Czechoslovakia

1993-1995

Located along the Vltava river front, within walking distance of the National Theatre and other prominent cultural facilities, the site is one of only three in the historic district of central Prague in which new construction is being permitted. The building formerly on the site was destroyed accidentally by an American bomber during World War II. The corner's site adjacency to an unusually shaped public square calls for a twin tower scheme that makes a smooth transition from street to the street, whilst creating a strong visual focus. The massing strategy also establishes a sculptural dialogue appropriate to its urban context.

The programmatic elements of the building distribute the 55,000 square feet of commercial office building to best take advantage of its unique location and massing strategy. On the ground level, directly accessible from the river front and public square, is a café and two-hundred square metres of retail space. An additional 230 square metres of retail occupy the lower level. The office spaces occupy floors two to eight and are designed to fulfil the most rigorous requirements of the client. The spaces directly behind the twin towers are to be used as special offices or conference rooms. Finally, a proposed bar and twelve-seat restaurant occupy the top level of the building to take full advantage of the spectacular view of the Prague skyline, including a view of the castle.

The main exterior facade, overlooking the river bank, responds to the rich textures and scale of the adjacent row of houses. Its staggered windows and horizontal striations gradually break into a wave pattern which relates to the undulating cornice lines of the lively neighbouring river front facades. It will be constructed of poured-in-place concrete with a plaster finish which is common to local Prague architecture.

The twin towers, one developed as a cylindrical solid volume, the other a tapering glass tower, are supported by a number of sculptural columns, creating a small covered entrance plaza for the offices above. The glass tower will be comprised of two layers of steel-supported glass curtain wall. The interior layer is the actual wall of the building with the sculptural outer layer acting as a screen for the office spaces underneath.

For this project, three-dimensional computer modelling played a key role in supplementing the traditional methods of documentation, bidding and quality control. This approach to three-dimensional computer modelling has been developed to link the design process more closely to fabrication and construction technologies as opposed to the imaging software more typically used by architects. The approach is intended to support and expand on a design process which relies heavily on building physical architectural study models and mock-ups.

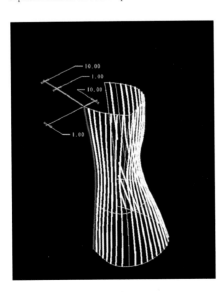

The Guggenheim Museum

Bilbao, Spain

1993-1997

The site is in a prominent location at the edge of the river bank where the main vehicular bridge crosses it, between the Museo de Bellas Artes and the City Hall. It is very close to the major business district of the city which was created on a nineteenth-century street grid. Connections to the city via tree-lined walkways and public spaces, plazas and the river front promenade are stressed in the scheme. Vistas from the city have been created so that the river is visible through the buildings. The scale of the expressed building parts relates to the existing buildings across the road and river, while the height of the atrium roof relates to the adjacent roof tops. The tall tower at the east end of the scheme 'captures' the bridge and makes it part of the building composition. Bilbao's river has been very important in its history and this is reflected in the introduction of the large areas of water in the project.

The programme for this design was for a 30,000 square metre world class modern and contemporary art museum including three different types of exhibition space: permanent collection; permanent site and specific installations; and temporary exhibition galleries. Additionally, the design includes other public facilities such as a 400-seat auditorium, a restaurant, a café, retail space, and a large central

atrium/orientation space which was envisioned to function almost as a public town square. Loading, parking, support, storage and administrative office space is also included, but because of the unique nature of the collection, the proportion of front-of-house to back-of-house space is about 2:1, as opposed to a more normal ratio of 1:2.

The programme of the museum is distributed on the site in several interconnected buildings, with a large central atrium space with its figural roof unifying the composition. Parking and back-of-house support facilities are located on the lowest levels adjacent to the truck dock and freight elevators.

The entry plaza leads into the central space which is surrounded on all four levels by galleries and has a large glass wall facing onto the river. The gallery buildings are designed to encourage the public ramps and stairs onto the roof terraces which provide views out over the river and city. The external circulation also provides opportunities for routing large crowds during 'blockbuster' shows outside the flow of normal circulation.

Gallery spaces are articulated as large rectangular volumes stacked upon one another, some of up to thirty metres width at the east end under the tall tower and column free space. Skylights are provided

via the sculptural roof forms above the temporary exhibition gallery building and a shaft through the west gallery. Gallery ceiling heights are generally maintained at six metres or more.

The auditorium is located on the entry plaza so that it can be used independently or as part of the museum. A restaurant is located at the northwest corner of the site overlooking the river and a café is located facing on the river walk. Another café or restaurant could be located on the roof of the auditorium and possibly within the sculpted form of the atrium roof. A 'look-out' or viewing platform could be created at the top of the east tower.

The major materials for the gallery buildings are limestone and sandblasted stainless steel, both of which are available locally. The structure will be a composite of concrete and steel frame with a tensile ring created to hold the atrium roof together. Mechanical systems are designed to maintain appropriate levels of control for the various uses. An access floor is used throughout the gallery spaces to allow flexibility for the infra-structure. Lighting will be a combination of indirect ambient light; direct exhibition light from a flush flat monopoint system; and filtered daylight from skylights and windows.

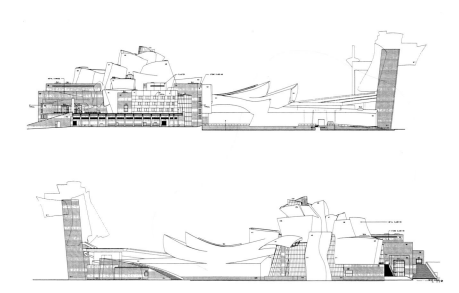

South elevation; North elevation

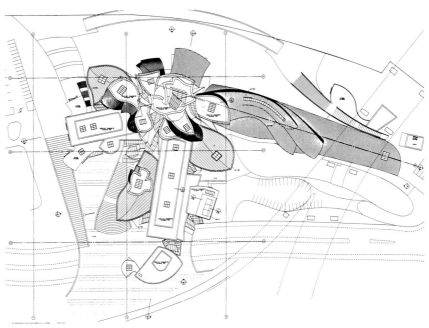

Roof plan

Selected Architecture 1964-1994

1964/1964-65
Danziger Studio/Residence, Hollywood, California

1965-83
Exhibit Installations, Los Angeles County Museum of Art, Los Angeles, California

1966/1966-67
Merriweather Post, Pavilion of Music, Columbia, Maryland

1968/1968
O'Neill Hayburn, San Juan Capistrano, California

1968/1969-72
Davis Studio/Residence, Malibu, California

1969/1972-74
The Rouse Company Headquarters Building, Columbia, Maryland

1971/1975-82
Hollywood Bowl Improvements, Hollywood, California

1972/1978-80
Santa Monica Place, Santa Monica, California

1973/1974-75
Concord Pavilion, Concord, California

1976
Jung Institute, Los Angeles, California

1977/1978-79
Cabrillo Marine Museum, San Pedro, California

1978
Familian Residence, Los Angeles, California

1978
Wagner Residence, Malibu, California

1978/1978
Gehry Residence, Santa Monica, California

1978/1980-91
Loyola Law School, Los Angeles, California

1978/1979
Spiller Residence, Venice, California

1979/1980-81
Indiana Avenue Studios, Venice, California

1979/1981-84
Benson House, Calabasas, California

1979/1980-81
House for a Film maker, Los Angeles, California

1981
Smith Residence, Los Angeles, California

1981/1982-84
Wosk Residence, Beverly Hills, California

1982/1983
The 'Temporary Contemporary', The Museum of Contemporary Art, Los Angeles, California

1982/1983-84
California Aerospace Museum and Theater, Los Angeles, California

1982/1983-84
Norton House, Venice, California

1982/1983-85
Rebecca's, Venice, California

1983/1985-86
Frances Goldwyn Hollywood Regional Branch Library, Hollywood, California

1983/1986-87
The Winton Residence Guest House, Wayzata, Minnesota

1983/1986-88
Simai-Peterson Residence, Thousand Oaks, California

1983/1985-89
Information and Computer Sciences/Engineering Research Laboratory and Engineering Center, UC Irvine, Irvine, California

1984
Médiathèque-Ventre d'Art Comtemporain, Nîmes, France

1984-85
Camp Good Times, The Santa Monica Mountains Conservancy Area, California

1984/1986-88
Edgemar Development, Santa Monica, California

1975/1986-91
Chiat/Day Main Street, Venice, California

1985-1986-88
360 Newbury Street, Boston, Massachusetts

1985/1988-89
Yale Psychiatric Institute, New Haven, Connecticut

1986
Turtle Creek Development, Dallas, Texas

1986/1986
Frank O. Gehry Retrospective Exhibition, Walker Art Center, Minneapolis, Minnesota

1986
Standing Glass Fish, Walker Art Center, Minneapolis, Minnesota

1986-1986-87
Fishdance Restaurant, Kobe, Japan

1986/1987-88
Chiat/Day Hampton Drive, Temporary Offices, Venice, California

1986/1987-89
Schnabel Residence, Brentwood, California

1986/1987-88
Sheet Metal Exhibition National Building Museum, Washington DC

1987-
Progressive Corporation, Corporate Headquarters, Cleveland, Ohio

1987
Penn Station/Madison Square Garden Redevelopment, New York, New York

1987/1988-89
Vitra International Furniture Manufacturing Facility and Design Museum, Weil am Rhein, Germany

1987/1988-89
Herman Miller Inc, Western Region Manufacturing & Distribution Facility, Rocklin, California

1987/1989-92
Iowa Advanced Technology, Laboratories Building, University of Iowa, Iowa City, Iowa

1988/1988
Chiat/Day Toronto, Toronto, Ontario, Canada

1988/1990-92
Entertainment Center at Eurodisneyland, Paris, France

1988/1991-94
American Center, Paris, France

1988/1992-94
New Headquarters for Vitra International, AG, Basel, Switzerland

1988 (competition)
1989 (project)/1992-97
Walt Disney Concert Hall, Los Angeles, California

1989/1991-92
Villa Olympica, Barcelona, Spain

1990/1991-93
University of Minnesota Art and Teaching Museum, Minneapolis, Minnesota

1990/1991-92
University of Toledo Art Building, Toledo, Ohio

1991/1993-95
Guggenheim Museum, Bilbao, Spain

1992/1995-96
Nationale-Nederlanden Office Building, Prague Czechoslovakia

Frank and Berta Gehry